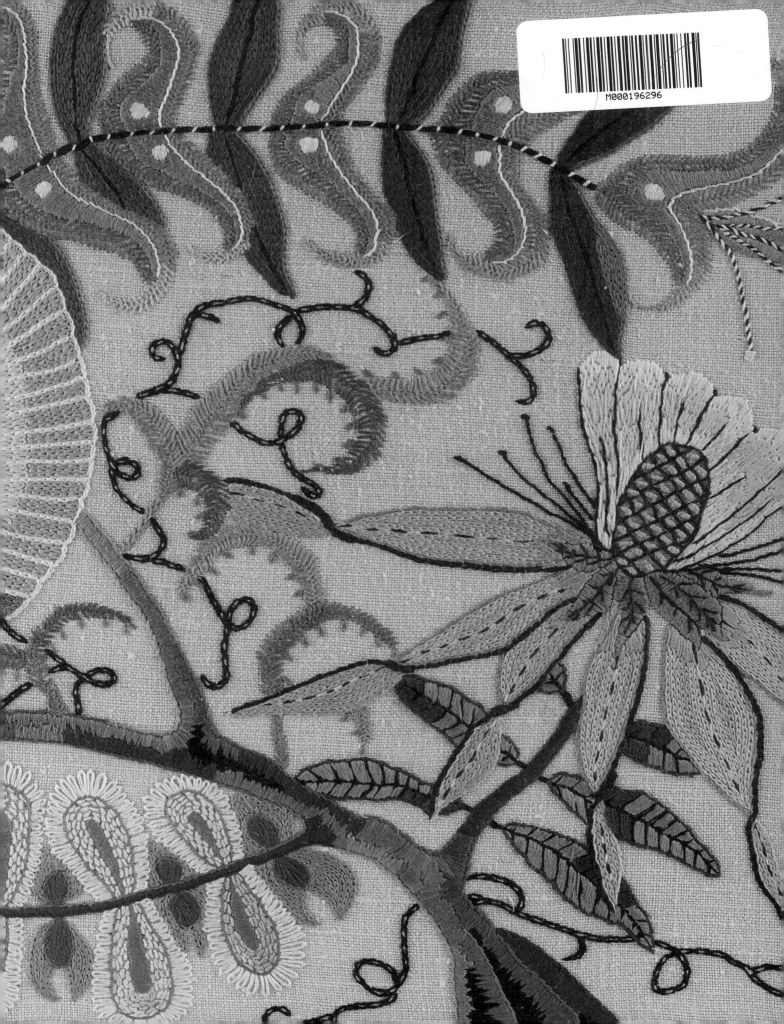

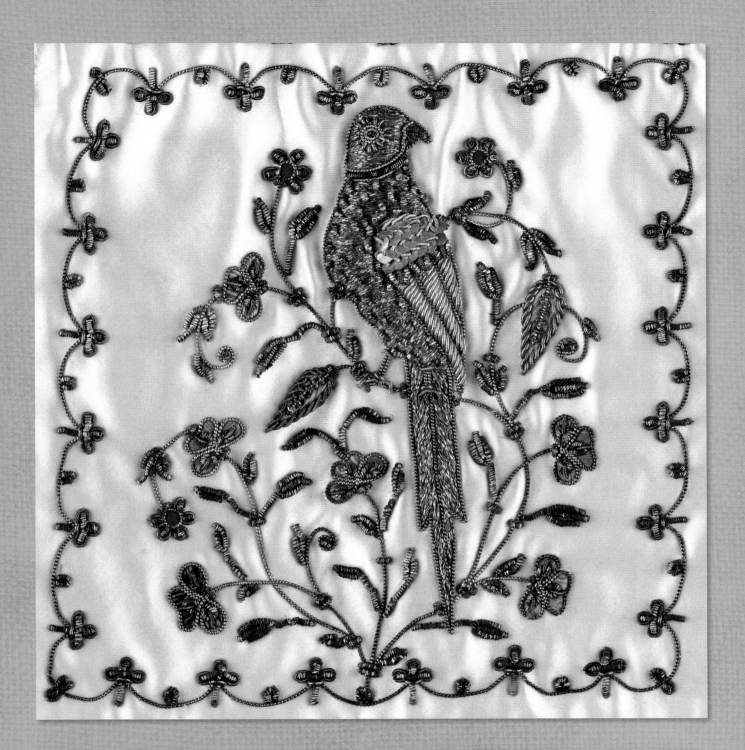

EMBROIDERED TREASURES
BIRDS

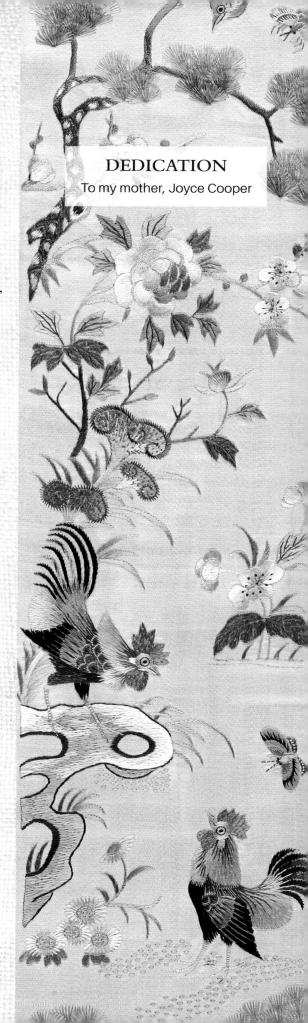

First published in 2018

Search Press Limited
Wellwood, North Farm Road,
Tunbridge Wells, Kent TN2 3DR

Text copyright © Dr Annette Collinge 2018

Photographs by Paul Bricknell
Photographs and design copyright © Search Press Ltd 2018

ISBN: 978-1-78221-132-7

Printed in China through Asia Pacific Offset

Photographs
Cover image: Chinese pheasants, page 86.
Previous page: Metal thread beadwork, page 73.
Right: Cockerel sleeve band, page 53.
Opposite: Silk embroidery seat cover, page 122.

DEDICATION
To my mother, Joyce Cooper

ACKNOWLEDGEMENTS

My thanks go to my family and friends for their support and
encouragement; the members of Willow Workshop; the Woking
Evening Branch of the Embroiderers' Guild and Dorking Branch of
the Embroiderers' Guild. In particular, to Catherine Sprowl, Marion
Brookes and to Sheila Philpot, who took her copy of my first book to
Sri Lanka so that I could sign it.

In addition, to Will Phillips, keeper of Social History at Bucks County
Museum, for getting out pieces from the Collection for photography,
and his volunteers for putting them away again; to Pat Tempest
from the Embroiderers' Guild for her help in editing the proofs of this
book and to Chris Berry for advice on 17th century stitches.

Thanks also to the team at Search Press.

EMBROIDERED TREASURES
BIRDS

Exquisite Needlework of the Embroiderers' Guild Collection

DR ANNETTE COLLINGE

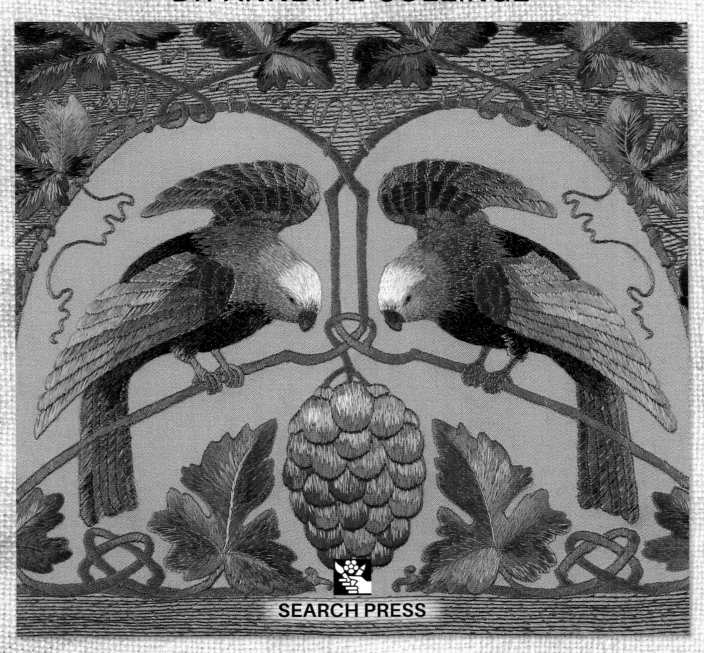

SEARCH PRESS

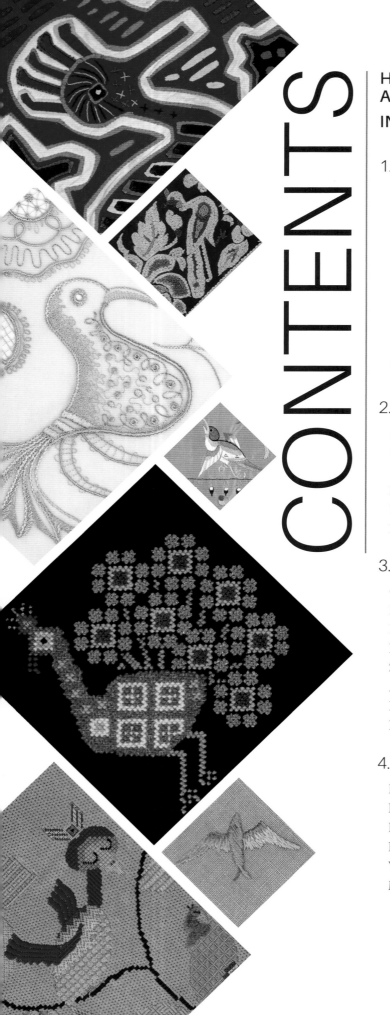

CONTENTS

HISTORY OF THE EG
AND ITS COLLECTION

The Embroiderers' Guild was formed in 1906 from the desire of a small group of enthusiasts to improve the quality of design and technique among embroiderers who, they felt, had become slaves to the published chart and printed canvas, and rarely attempted their own unique designs.

This group of 16 women were graduates from the Royal School of Art Needlework, which later became the Royal School of Needlework. The catchy title they came up with was The Society of Certificated Embroideresses of the Royal School of Art Needlework, but this was changed after the First World War to the Embroiderers' Guild, a much friendlier title.

The Embroiderers' Guild Collection is nearly as old as the Embroiderers' Guild itself. Our first president was Louisa Pesel, who was elected after the First World War and it was due to her involvement with the Women's Institute (WI) that the seeds of the Collection were sown. At a lecture she gave at a WI conference, people enquired if the examples of embroidery she had brought along could be borrowed.

Before long, a committee was in place at the Embroiderers' Guild headquarters to deal with 'model' or example boxes of embroideries and

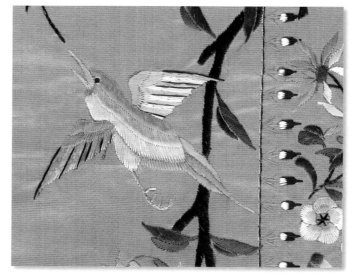

their distribution to the members on a regular basis, to improve their knowledge of design and technique. Members were allowed to handle the embroideries and encouraged to examine them closely. This resulted in an ongoing need to launder, repair and replace the existing embroideries.

Members made and donated embroideries to the model boxes and these continue today in the form of folios, which are available for members to borrow; the contents cover many aspects of embroidery. The original model boxes are thought to have been small boxes rather like laundry boxes, fastened with a leather strap. Current folios are enclosed in bright yellow folders. They now represent our educational resource but are not part of the Embroiderers' Guild Collection.

The Permanent Collection started as a result of donations that were too large or valuable to be put in a model box. HM Queen Mary donated large hangings and costume pieces and Lady Mary Cayley donated valuable 17th century pieces. Travellers and scholars also donated their collections of international embroideries and so the Embroiderers' Guild Permanent Collection was formed.

The Collection developed slowly and it was not until 1971 that the first catalogue was produced, when the number of embroideries listed was 114. There are now nearly 6,000 beautiful embroidered pieces in the Embroiderers' Guild Collection.

The Collection has seen a number of homes in London, including Grosvenor Street and its second most well-known home, Wimpole Street. When the lease ran out at Wimpole Street, the Collection had a number of temporary homes, including Greycoat Place where, it is said, the Collection was stored above a chip shop.

The most famous address was an apartment at Hampton Court Palace, where the Collection was stored to museum standards for the first time. This was followed by EG House in Walton-upon-Thames and currently the Collection is housed at Bucks County Museum Resource Centre near Aylesbury, UK.

Members have always been very protective of their Collection and small hitches such as world wars have not posed a problem, as members simply took the Collection home with them to be looked after until conditions improved.

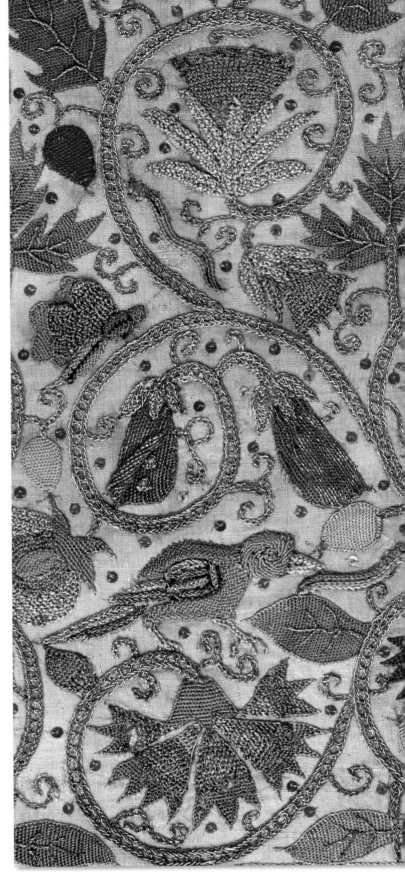

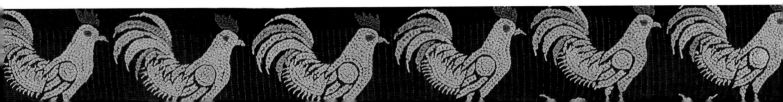

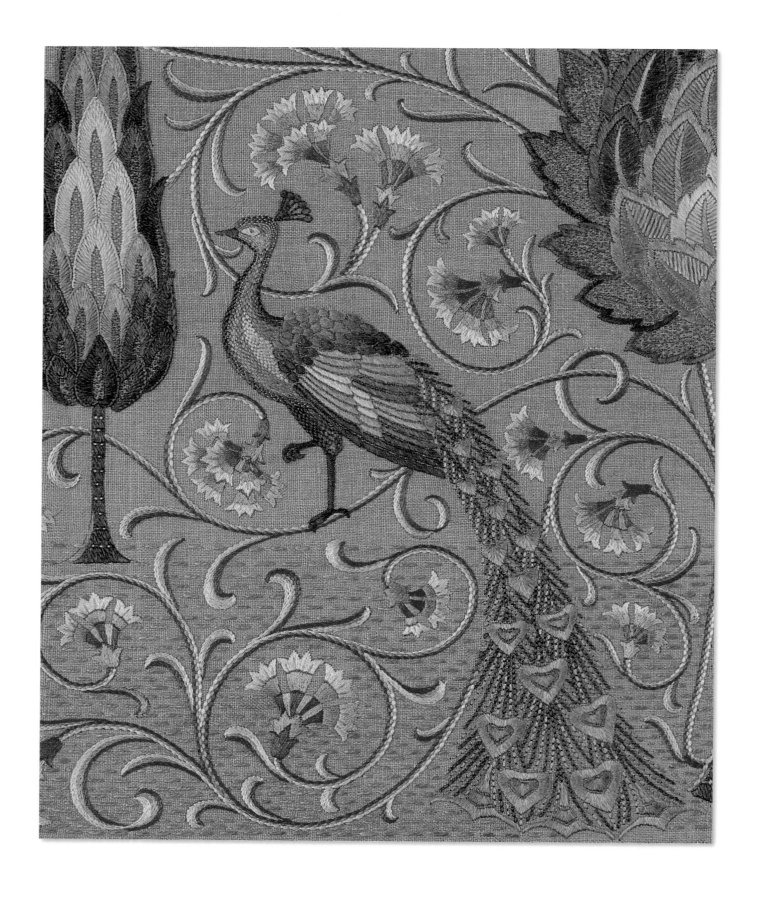
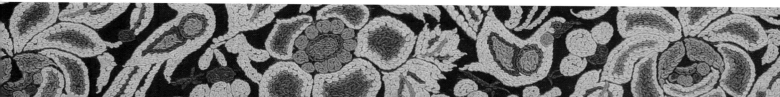

British embroideries form the main body of the Collection, with the earliest pieces from the 16th century. Sadly, there are only a few of these, but samples increase in numbers through each century to the present day. The earliest pieces in the Collection are not embroideries, but Coptic weavings, which were preserved in dry, sandy graves dating back to the 6th to 10th centuries.

The 20th century sees the largest number of pieces in the Collection, ranging from domestic embroideries and pictures, often made from hot iron transfer designs, to the inception of textile art in the mid to late part of the century, when the Embroiderers' Guild specifically collected contemporary embroidery and work by textile artists.

Various Embroiderers' Guild members in the past were travellers and scholars and, through their donations, we have extensive numbers of embroideries from China, India, Turkey, Greece and Eastern Europe. Less well represented are Japan, Scandinavia and the Americas.

Originally, the Collection was solely for the membership and this is still the case today. Membership of the Embroiderers' Guild entitles members to see and photograph any piece from the Collection. Travelling exhibitions enable us to reach members further afield. Smaller pieces are distributed among the folios and these are constantly added to by donations and bequests.

We continue to have very supportive members working today, who have donated their artwork to the Collection. These pieces are supplemented by the purchase of contemporary textile art, keeping the Collection up to date and relevant to the present day.

Dr Annette Collinge

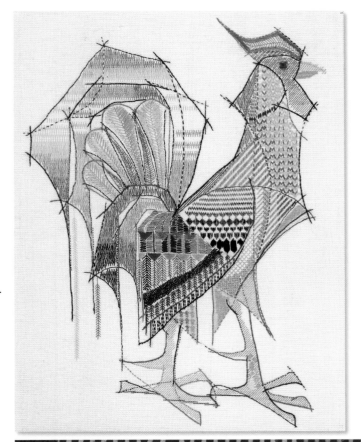

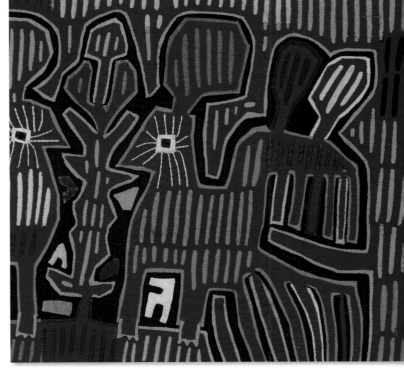

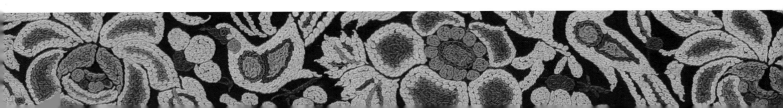

INTRODUCTION

When primitive humans first found they could use a sharpened stick to pierce animal skins and thread fibres through the holes made, they would also have been aware of the birds in their environment. Using the surrounding flora and fauna as inspiration for the decoration of clothing followed many generations later.

In the 16th century, plants were illustrated in 'herbals', which were among the first printed books. Natural history books that included birds were also available. The Bayeux tapestry from the 11th century portrays many birds and by the 17th century, birds including owls, birds of prey, peacocks, herons and songbirds can be found, together with the mythical phoenix.

Birds in early embroidery never seem to have enjoyed the popularity that flowers have, often appearing as tiny additions to floral designs or having ecclesiastical significance, such as the dove and pelican. I could speculate on why this might be. Perhaps it is because flowers are more static – they are growing all around, whereas birds are constantly in the air or too far away to make a detailed study. Early illustrations of birds are often fanciful, with unlikely colour combinations and elaborate wing and tail feathers.

Birds lend themselves to fine embroidery and very early embroideries were limited by the fabric available at the time. Loosely woven linen fabric did not encourage fine work, whereas fine silk and other closely woven fabrics were suited to intricate designs, the use of fine threads and as a base for metal thread embroidery. This is particularly so in China and many of the birds in our Collection come from that part of the world, beautifully and intricately embroidered.

We have to wait until the 18th century before birds become significant features of embroidery. A comment in *Weldons Flower Embroidery* states that

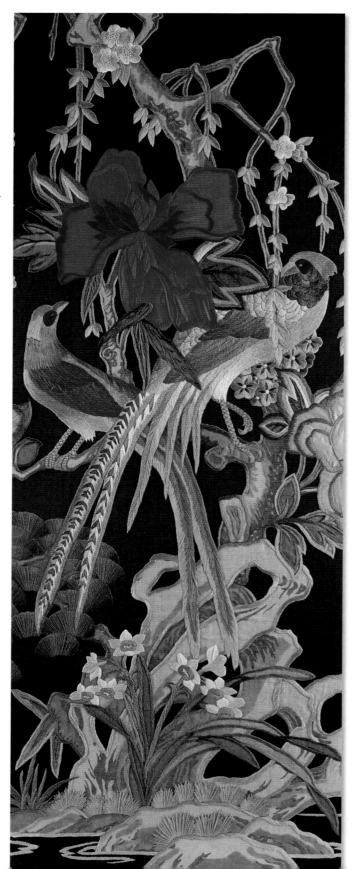

even when a bird of sombre hue is being copied, the colour should be kept as bright as possible without departing too far from nature.

In the 19th century, *Birds of America*[1] and *A Century of Birds from the Himalaya Mountains*[2] were published in London and might have been a rich source of inspiration for the embroiderer. Travellers and explorers brought back bird specimens, which were stuffed for display and study. In the UK in Victorian times, there would have been game birds to study, but the most popular birds for embroidery worldwide are peacocks, parrots and storks or cranes.

The earliest depictions of birds in the Embroiderers' Guild Collection are from the 16th century, mostly rather insignificant birds in Italian lace. The earliest examples in this book come from the 17th century and continue to the 21st century. In the 20th century, new approaches to embroidery led to embroidery as an art form and bird designs gained favour with contemporary textile artists. Of course, beautiful birds are being stitched today using traditional techniques and these represent a significant gap in the Embroiderers' Guild Collection.

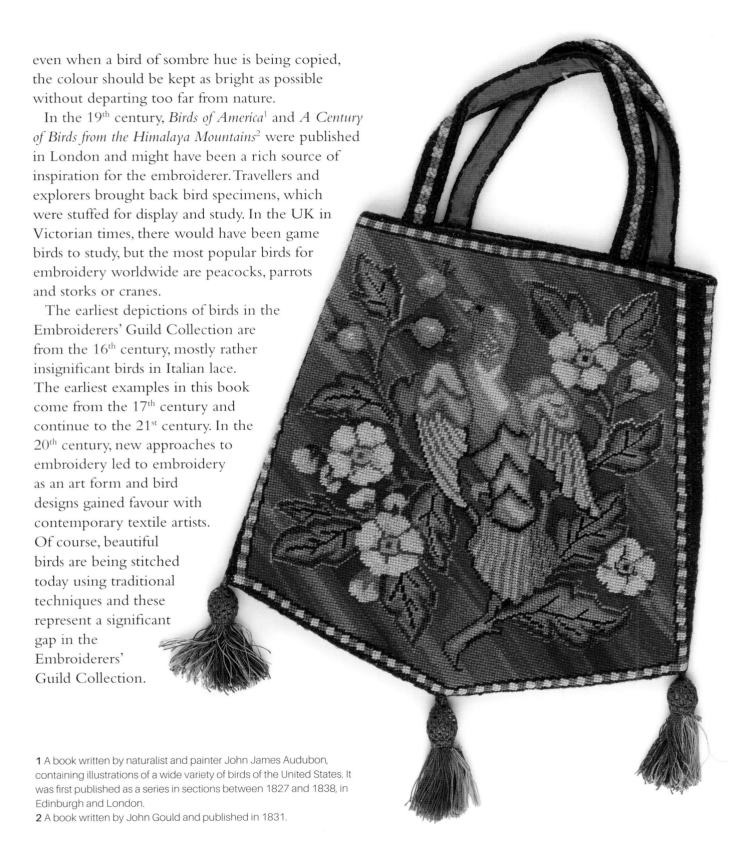

1 A book written by naturalist and painter John James Audubon, containing illustrations of a wide variety of birds of the United States. It was first published as a series in sections between 1827 and 1838, in Edinburgh and London.
2 A book written by John Gould and published in 1831.

EMBROIDERY IN MONOCHROME

Monochrome embroidery is embroidery in a single colour. It can be very fine and delicate or bold and textural. Most embroidery in the Collection that comes under this category is in black or white thread, but other colours can be found and blackwork embroidery has a tradition of specific stitches.

Looking at the birds in the Collection, there are none that can be described as traditional blackwork and this chapter concentrates on traditional whitework embroidery featuring birds and other examples where the birds are in one colour, but might be equally at home in other categories.

The earliest bird in this chapter is an example of 17th century crewelwork in red thread on a linen background and the latest, the 20th century cockerel stitched by Barbara Snook, in white thread on a red background. Other birds are stitched in gold and silk threads, herons in felt appliqué and a hooked rug from Labrador.

Traditional whitework is represented by *tele tirata* and *buratto* lace from Italy. Embroidery on muslin and a pair of minutely stitched confronting birds complete the chapter.

CREWELWORK PANEL

TECHNIQUE: crewel embroidery
DATE: mid 17th century
PLACE of origin: England
SIZE: 33 x 28cm (13 x 11in)

Popularly known as crewel embroidery, the word 'crewel' refers to the wool yarn used, rather than the style of embroidery. This charming little bird, with a twig in his beak and perched on a twig with two berries, is part of a fragment in red wool on linen twill fabric and was probably part of a wall hanging, bed hanging or cover.

In the 17th century, houses were draughty and many embroidered textiles were used to block out those draughts. Early crewel embroidery was usually monochrome and the most popular colour was red. Later in

the 17th century, crewel embroidery became more colourful and the designs more elaborate. Unlike counted thread work where the design is made by counting threads, crewel embroidery is a freestyle technique where designs were drawn on to the fabric.

In this example, the drawn design can be seen in places as well as needle holes, where threads have been lost. Stitches used are not specific to crewel embroidery but are traditional stitches; stem stitch, chain stitch and split stitch. Seeding stitches were often used to create shading by spacing the stitches close together and further apart. The popularity of crewel embroidery during the reign of King James 1st (1566–1625) led to the term 'Jacobean embroidery', which is still used today for crewelwork designs.

Embroiderers' Guild number: EG1981

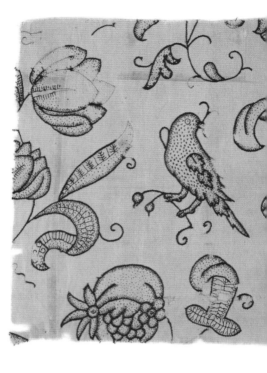

CONFRONTING BIRDS

TECHNIQUE: hand embroidery; whitework
DATE: late 19th century
PLACE of origin: Great Britain
SIZE: 12 x 11cm (4¾ x 4¼in)

This pair of birds facing each other, known as Confronting Birds, is stitched in cotton thread on fine muslin. The design is derived from a design by C.F.A. Voysey (1857–1941), who was a leading British architect and textile designer. The chubby little birds with their alert eyes are embroidered against an Art Nouveau floral background. Mainly stitched in very fine satin stitch, there are also eyelets and seeding stitches. In the EG catalogue, this is described as a fragment. At some point the edges have been hemmed. There is no indication of what its original purpose was.

Maker: Miss Gray
Embroiderers' Guild number: EG5680

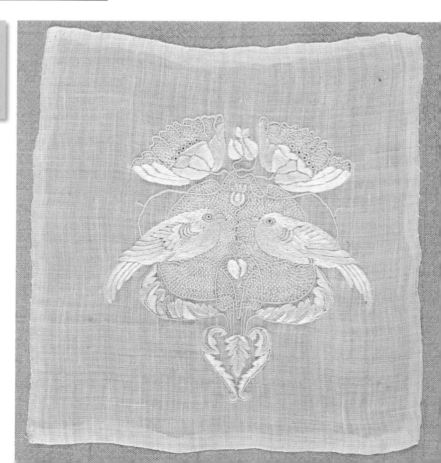

14

DRAWN THREAD WORK

TECHNIQUE: tele tirata
DATE: early 20th century
PLACE of origin: Italy (Sicily)
SIZE: 76 x 68cm (30 x 26¾in)

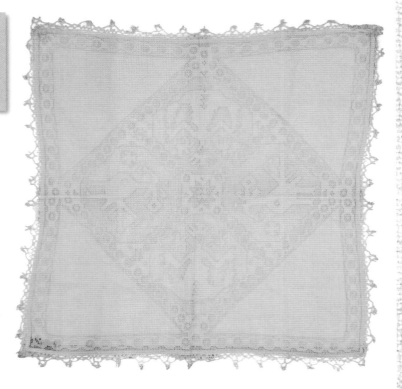

The term for this drawn thread work is *tele tirata*, an Italian form of drawn thread work that originated in medieval times and continued for many years after. This rather strange bird might be a stylized peacock. To create this bird, threads are cut and drawn from the ground fabric which, in this case, is linen, leaving a grid of threads. These threads are then overcast using a self-coloured linen thread to create a firm grid or mesh. The design is created by areas of ground fabric that do not have cut and drawn threads. This cloth has a central diamond-shaped motif with two stylized birds and two mermaids with double tails, holding a tail in each hand. We shall come across this design later in the book when we look at embroideries from Crete. The cloth has a needle lace border.

Embroiderers' Guild number: EG5285

BURATTO LACE

TECHNIQUE: buratto work
DATE: 16–17th century
PLACE of origin: Italy
SIZE: 186 x 9cm (73¼ x 3½in)

Embroiderers' Guild number: L1589

I call this design the pompous peacocks, confronting each other along a border strip of *buratto* lace from Italy.

Buratto is a 17th century needle lace technique. A special loom is used on which weft threads are crossed and recrossed round the warp threads, anchoring them in place. This creates a net foundation on which the design is darned, stretched on a frame. The technique usually produced narrow bands, as with this piece. *Buratto* lace is usually white, but coloured *buratto* is found, although rarely. We are lucky enough to have examples of coloured *buratto* lace in the Embroiderers' Guild Collection.

The term *buratto* is derived from the word 'bura', which means coarse cloth. It is also noted as a technique which produces a very similar front and back. This piece has an L number, which indicates that it is part of the Embroiderers' Guild lace collection.

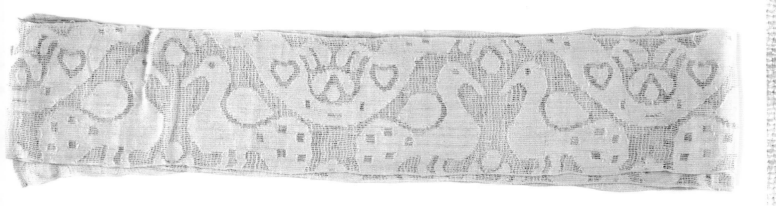

EMBROIDERY ON MUSLIN

TECHNIQUE: whitework
DATE: 18th century
PLACE of origin: Great Britain or India
SIZE: 55 x 48.5cm (21¾ x 19in)

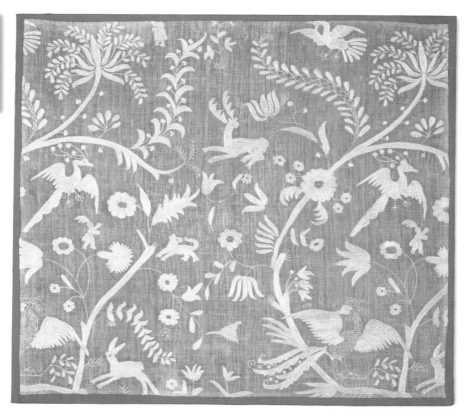

This example of fine embroidery on muslin is rather like the confronting birds seen on page 14. In this case, the piece is thought to be an apron or petticoat fragment. It is not known where it was made, but Great Britain or India are possibilities and, as an apron, it would be more typical of Indian rather than British costume.

The stitching is worked in cotton thread and includes surface darning, stem stitch and some pulled thread and whipped stitches. This embroidery is typical of 'chinoiserie' or Chinese style. It was very popular in the 18th century when trade with China and Eastern Asia was thriving.

It was the global phenomenon of the 18th century with versions produced in many countries, including India. Designs were flamboyant, asymmetrical and often portrayed nature in the form of birds and animals. It was all about leisure and pleasure and the picture European minds had of Chinese culture.

Muslin is a cotton fabric made in a wide range of weights, from delicate sheers as in this example to coarse sheeting. The name comes from the city of Mosul, in Iraq, where it is thought it was first manufactured.

India has a culture of embroidery on muslin, often made for the European market and embracing chinoiserie style. For this reason, we do not know whether this piece was made in India or Great Britain.

Embroiderers' Guild number: EG1587

A STRUTTING COCKEREL

TECHNIQUE: hand embroidery
DATE: mid 20th century
PLACE of origin: Great Britain
SIZE: 20 x 28cm (8 x 11in)

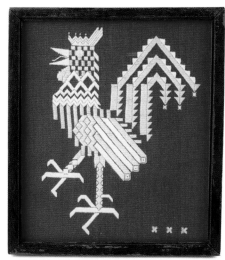

On to the 20th century and a strutting cockerel by Barbara Snook on bright red evenweave linen and counted satin stitch in white cotton thread. This piece is taken from a design from Aleppo in Syria. It is part of a large number of embroideries in the EG Collection by Barbara Snook. Barbara was a tutor and author who, on retiring from teaching, travelled widely (including to Peru) before package holidays came about. She made drawings of natural forms, which she used in her designs. She wrote many embroidery books, especially for children.

Barbara Snook's work was found in the Collection with 'T' or temporary numbers. These were given permanent accession numbers in 2014.

Maker: Barbara Snook (1913-1977)
Gifted by: Jean Carter
Embroiderers' Guild number: EG2014.3

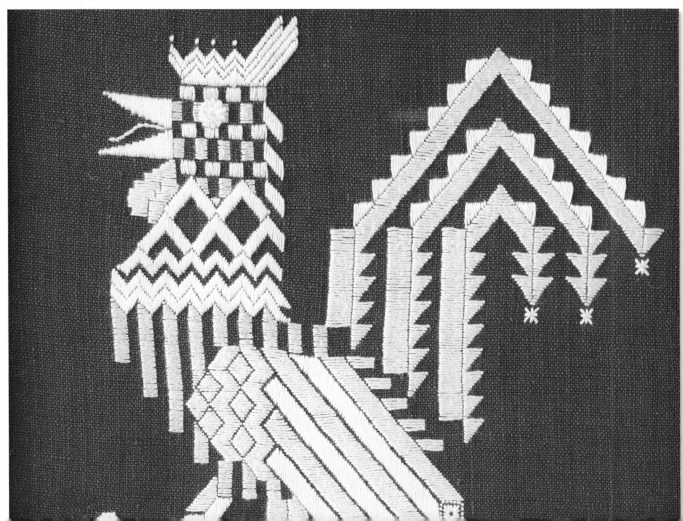

FELT APPLIQUÉ

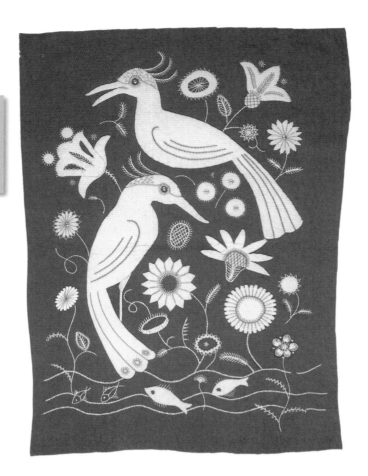

TECHNIQUE: felt appliqué
DATE: 1920
PLACE of origin: Great Britain
SIZE: 47 x 63cm (18½ x 24¾in)

Here we have two beautiful herons, surrounded by flowers and standing in a river, complete with fish. The technique is felt appliqué with surface embroidery.

This piece is made entirely from felt with white felt birds applied to a grey felt background, and the embroidery details are in grey cotton thread. Simple stitches are used to enhance the design. It is the simplicity of this technique that makes the design stand out. Compare it with Barbara Snook's cockerel (page 17), which uses only one stitch for a bold effect. The maker, Anne Haywood, studied at the Royal College of Art and went on to be a tutor at art schools and the Women's Institute in the southeast of England.

Maker: Anne Haywood (1898-1966)
Embroiderers' Guild number: EG5472

METAL THREAD CUSHION

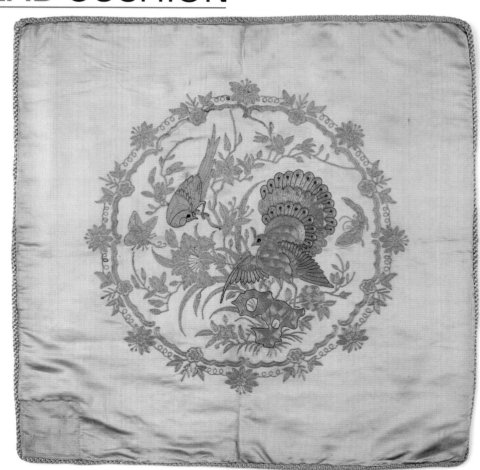

TECHNIQUE: metal thread embroidery
DATE: 19th century
PLACE of origin: Japan
SIZE: 54 x 55cm (21¼ x 21½in)

This silk embroidery from Japan is one of very few bird embroideries in the Collection that is entirely stitched in couched gold thread. It is a cushion cover of pale blue silk, not totally monochrome, as red and lilac silk threads are used for couching. This technique is used because metal threads are not suited to surface embroidery, as they have a tendency to unravel when pulled through cloth. Instead, threads are laid on the surface of the fabric and couched in place with finer threads. Is the bird a peacock? Or perhaps it is a rather grand turkey.

Embroiderers' Guild number: EG4526

18

RUG HOOKING

TECHNIQUE: rug hooking
DATE: 1929
PLACE of origin: North America (Labrador)
SIZE: 56 x 40cm (22 x 15¾in)

This is called 'Night Scene with Canada Geese' and it is a small rug. Loops of wool yarn are pulled through a stiff base which, in this example, is hessian (burlap). This is achieved with a crochet-like hook mounted in a wooden handle. The technique has been around for hundreds of years and is still popular today.

This rug is recorded as coming from Dr Grenfell's Mission in Labrador. The Grenfell Mission was a medical and religious mission founded in 1892 by Sir Wilfred Grenfell to help the poor. People came from around the world to help at the mission, including Scotland and England. The mission was famous for its hessian (burlap) rugs, which were sold for the benefit of the mission. These Grenfell rugs are highly prized by folk art collectors and it seems we are lucky enough to have one in the Embroiderers' Guild Collection. In 2005, the mission became the International Grenfell Association.

Embroiderers' Guild number: EG5305

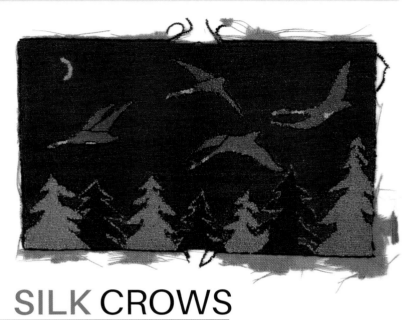

SILK CROWS

TECHNIQUE: silk embroidery
DATE: 19th century
PLACE of origin: Japan
SIZE: 44.5 x 21cm (17½ x 8¼in)

This is one of my favourite embroideries from Japan. The cream silk background is painted to look like the sky with crows in dark blue silk threads, worked in satin stitch. It is the simplicity of the design that appeals to me and the limited stitches. Compare this embroidery with Barbara Snook's cockerel (page 17), Anne Haywood's herons (page 18) and the 17th century crewelwork bird at the beginning of the chapter (page 14). All four stand out as something achievable by embroiderers today.

Embroiderers' Guild number: EG1982.130.20

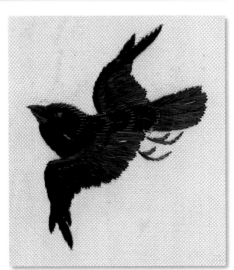

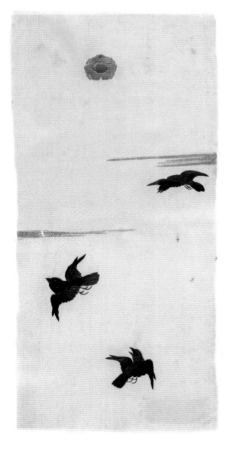

THE USE OF
METAL THREAD

The technique of metal thread embroidery goes back many centuries and its use was originally in ecclesiastical and heraldic embroidery, when it was carried out by professional workers. Today, most metal thread work is stitched using synthetic threads, which are available for both hand and machine embroidery. The earliest examples utilizing metal thread in the Embroiderers' Guild Collection are from the 16th century, but examples featuring birds date from later where metal threads are usually combined with silk embroidery.

Peacocks feature strongly in Indian metal thread embroidery and have given me the opportunity to introduce beetle wings which, although not metal thread, have a metallic lustre. Chinese metal thread work is represented by a 'rank badge'.

CHINESE RANK BADGE

TECHNIQUE: metal thread embroidery
DATE: late 19th century
PLACE of origin: China
SIZE: 21.5 x 23cm (8½ x 9in)

This is a rank badge from China. These badges represented the authority and status of the wearer. They would be sewn on to ceremonial robes, one on the back and one on the front of the garment.

There were nine ranks in the Chinese court, divided into military and civil. Military badges depicted animals, but the more highly regarded civil badges depicted birds. It is said this was because birds could fly nearer to heaven. The bird represents the court official looking towards the sun. The bird stands on the rocks of the earth, above the seas and surrounded by a sky filled with precious objects. When worn on the back of a garment, the bird faces the wearer's left shoulder and, on the front, his right shoulder.

This rank badge is a symbol of the third civil rank. Gold and silver threads are couched down with coloured silks. The badge is packed with embroidery. The bird motif has been worked separately and then applied to the badge. So much symbolism and a story to tell in such a small embroidery.

Embroiderers' Guild number: EG1982.62.1

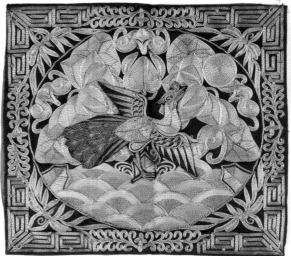

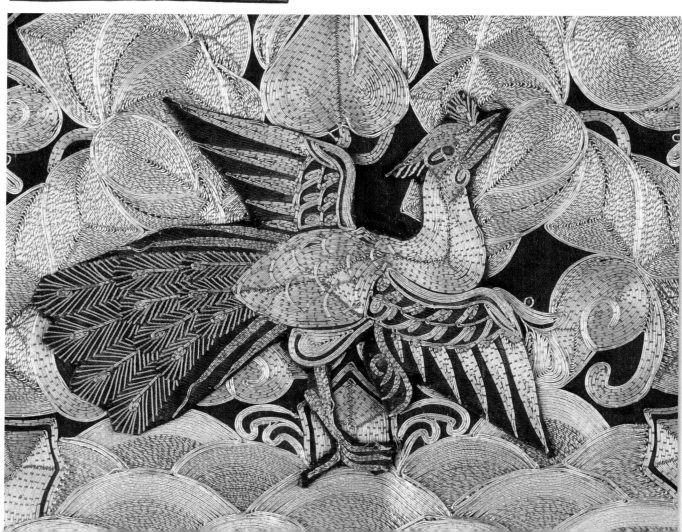

PEACOCK PANEL

TECHNIQUE: metal thread embroidery

DATE: late 19th century

PLACE of origin: India

SIZE: 51 x 89cm (20 x 35in)

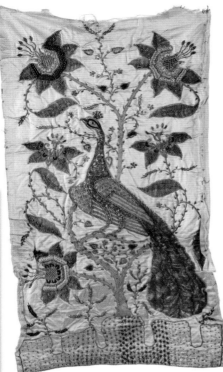

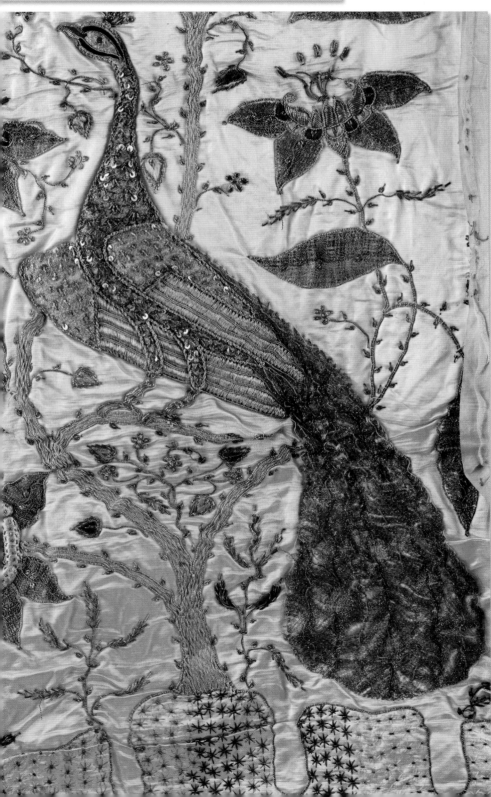

In this piece an elaborate peacock is perching in a tree surrounded by flowers. The background is yellow silk and the peacock is padded, with metal threads couched down over the padding. The effect is sumptuous with silk threads and sequins adding to the richness of the embroidery. It is described as a cover. In India, covers were made for many purposes; for cushions and bolsters, tables, seats, bedding, clothes and even food.

The peacock is indigenous to India and has been part of Indian art and culture since ancient times. It has symbolic significance as a protector and herald of prosperity, royalty, fertility, love and joy. Its noisy cry, often considered an irritation to those living nearby, is in fact a cry of joy when it encounters a meeting of lovers. This piece is described as an untraced find in our catalogue, which means that it has no provenance; we do not know who donated it, or when.

Embroiderers' Guild number: EG4893

SATIN CUSHION COVER

TECHNIQUE: metal thread embroidery

DATE: 19th century

PLACE of origin: India

SIZE: 58 x 56cm (23 x 22in)

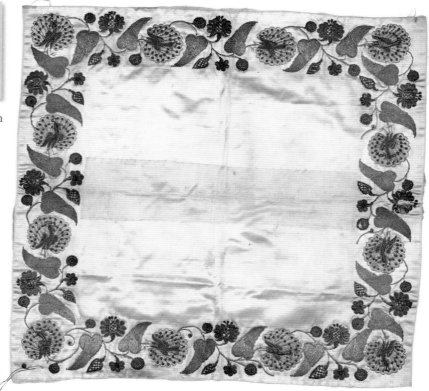

This cover from India is probably a cushion cover. Twelve beautiful peacocks are depicted in a border, perching on twining stems with leaves and flowers. The cover, made of cream satin, is stitched with couched gold threads.

Notice how the satin fabric gleams, complementing the richness of the embroidery. The body of each peacock is padded, with the gold threads couched over the padding to make the peacock stand out. Blue silk threads in straight stitches are used for the tail, which are perfect for portraying feathers. The god Krishna, the divine lover, is always depicted with a peacock feather in his hair. Notice how the leaves and flowers surrounding the peacocks are all gold. The use of padding and coloured silk threads on the peacock emphasizes the importance of the peacock in Indian culture.

Embroiderers' Guild number: EG3252

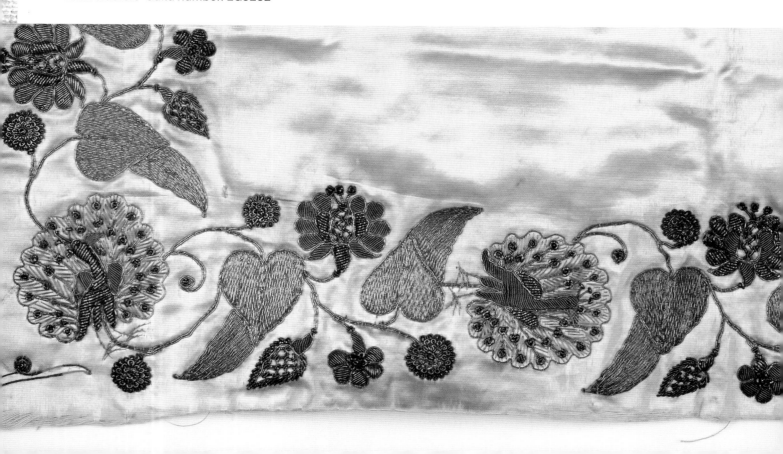

BEETLE WING COVER

TECHNIQUE: metal thread embroidery

DATE: 19th century

PLACE of origin: India

SIZE: 53.5 x 57.5cm (21 x 22¾in)

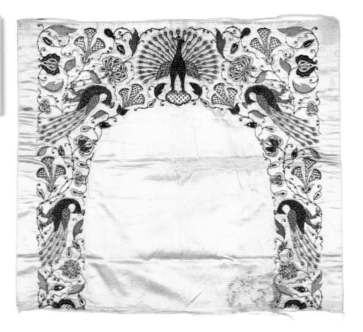

Sadly, this cover has been cut in half. It was originally rectangular in shape with a peacock border, leaving a clear rectangle of fabric in the centre. At one end is a beautiful peacock with its tail displayed and on either side, four peacocks with their tails folded. The birds are surrounded by leaves and flowers and the embroidery is worked in metal thread and silk thread.

What is interesting about this cover is the addition of beetle wings, which is a technique common in 19th century Europe and America, but especially India. We have several examples of beetle wing embroidery in the Embroiderers' Guild Collection and all of them are from India. The technique uses the iridescent, emerald green wing cases of a wood-boring species of beetle. The wing cases are surprisingly hard and durable and are attached to fabric by a crisscross of threads to hold the wing in place, or by stitching through holes bored through the wings. In some examples, the wings are broken up and fragments are attached to fabric. Look at the central peacock on this piece and beyond the orange-brown leaves on either side of the tail, you will see beetle wings.

Embroiderers' Guild number: EG4892

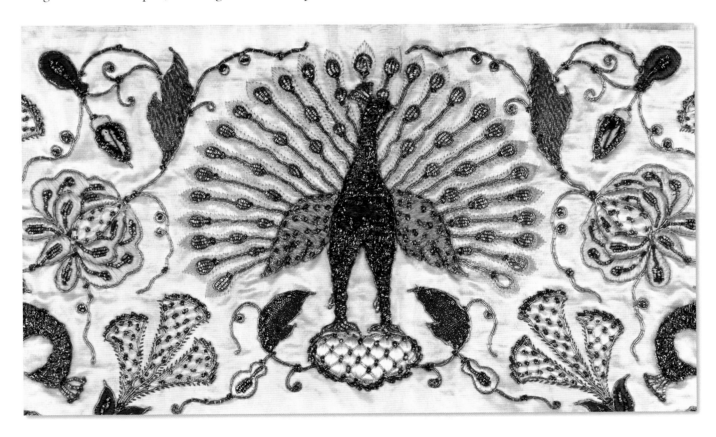

PEA POD PANEL

TECHNIQUE: hand embroidery
DATE: early 17th century
PLACE of origin: Great Britain
SIZE: 42.5 x 22.5cm (16¾ x 8¾in)

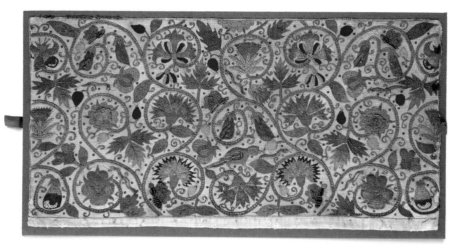

This beautiful example of early 17th century embroidery is known as the pea pod panel, but if you look beneath the pea pods there is a little bird, perching on a carnation as big as itself and striding towards an equally outsized caterpillar. Look at that alert eye. The centre of the bird is a woven wheel in silver metal thread, surrounded by spirals of silk thread, which are followed in to the head.

The body of the bird is in silk thread and trellis stitch – a very popular stitch in Elizabethan embroidery – and is a knotted needle lace stitch. Reverse chain stitch is used on the bird's legs and the metal thread wings and tail feathers are in plaited braid stitch. At first glance,

the beak appears to be reverse stitch but is more likely to be Ceylon stitch, which produces a tighter stitch.

This panel was donated to the Embroiderers' Guild on the closure of the Needlework Development Scheme (see page 34). This was started in 1934 by four Scottish art colleges, to encourage education in needlework and embroidery. Examples of embroidery, usually

domestic, were made for the scheme but historic and international pieces were also donated. This is one of the historic pieces. When the Scheme closed in 1960, the collection was distributed among several organizations, including the Embroiderers' Guild.

Gifted by: Needlework Development Scheme in 1962
Embroiderers' Guild number: EG1982.79

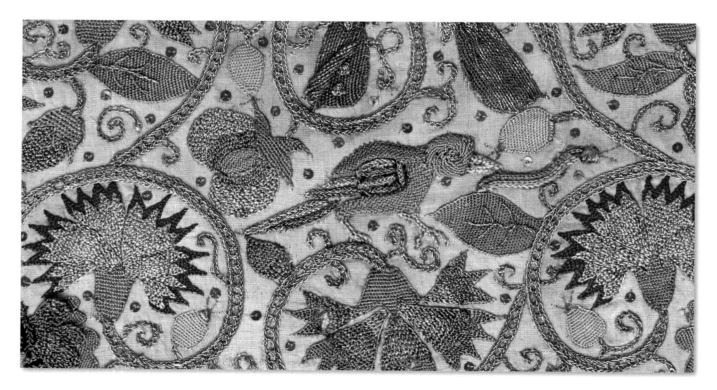

DECORATIVE PEACOCK PANEL

TECHNIQUE: metal thread embroidery
DATE: early 20th century
PLACE of origin: India (Delhi)
SIZE: 57 x 67cm (22½ x 26½in)

Depicted on a panel of ivory silk satin are two peacocks perching in flowering trees. The technique is metal thread embroidery with padded shapes, gold thread, silk thread and some areas of shiny silver purls.

This is another example of an untraced find, where we have no provenance. So, why is this panel considered to be 20th century and specifically from Delhi? Many Indian embroideries were made for the European market and a major centre for production was Delhi. The panel is decorative compared to the functional 19th century covers we have looked at and the flowers are stylized and might have been made to a perceived impression of what European flowers should look like. Of course, these criteria could apply to the earlier pieces, especially the one on page 23, which might be a panel rather than a cover. Identifying and dating embroidery where there is no provenance can be a very inexact science.

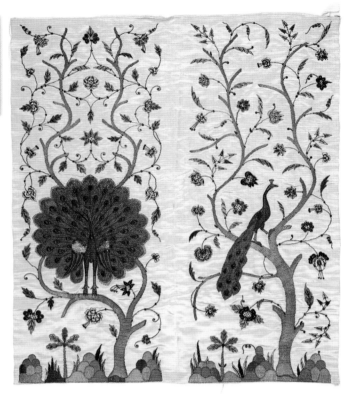

Embroiderers' Guild number: EG1248

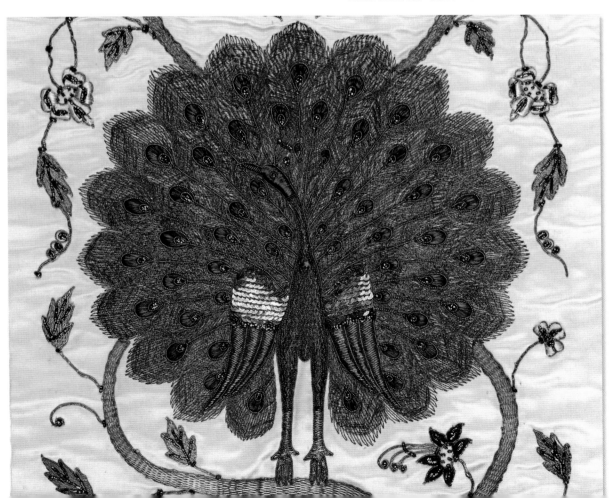

APPLIED
MATERIALS

In this chapter we look at techniques where fabric is used to convey a design onto other fabrics, by cutting out shapes in fabric and stitching them to a background; or by using random scraps of fabric to achieve the desired effect in contemporary textile art.

We are introduced to embroidery kits and hot iron transfer designs from the mid 20th century and the techniques of inlay and reverse appliqué.

Felt appliqué was particularly popular because of the ease with which the fabric can be drawn upon and cut out. We look at an example of textile art where felt appliqué has been used in a traditional way in a contemporary, original design.

COLLAGE OWL KIT

TECHNIQUE: appliqué, collage
DATE: 1970
PLACE of origin: Great Britain
SIZE: 45 x 45cm (17¾ x 17¾in)

This bird is undoubtedly an owl. To me, he looks slightly cross-eyed. In the 1970s and 1980s embroidery kits were very popular. The buyer took away from a shop, or ordered from a magazine, a bag containing everything needed to complete the design. All that was needed was to follow the instructions from a working chart on a ready-traced background fabric. Surface stitches were simple, straight stitches; the fabric shapes were felt and buttons and braids might be included in the kits to add interest.

This owl kit was priced at 53 shillings in 1970 and is described as a collage panel, simply entitled 'Owl'. It was a Penelope kit from W. M. Briggs and Co Ltd. Having seen an original kit of this owl, I can see that the artist has embellished her owl with extra embroidery, especially the wheels on the felt circles.

Maker: Pauline Webber
Embroiderers' Guild number: EG2014.40

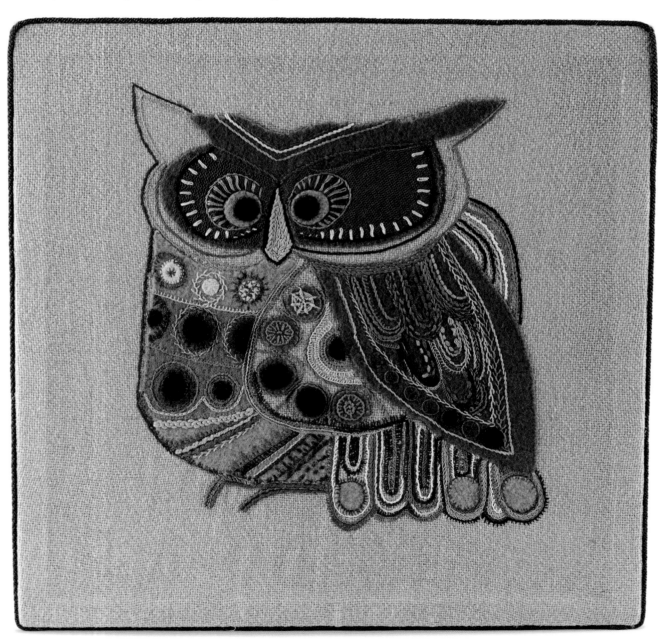

HOT IRON TRANSFER DESIGN

TECHNIQUE: appliqué

DATE: 20th century (1934)

PLACE of origin: Great Britain

SIZE: 97.5 x 58.5cm (38³/₈ x 23in)

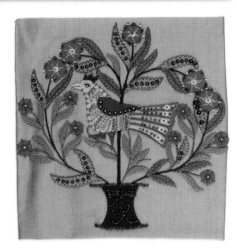

This colourful bird is a very English peacock, although some might say that it is rather rounded for a peacock and more like an elaborate hen. It is apparently sitting in a vase of flowers. It is worked from a hot iron transfer design and is one of my favourite pieces in the Embroiderers' Guild Collection. The big difference in this design compared with the owl, worked from a kit on the opposite page is that, with a transfer design, the embroiderer makes her own choice of fabrics and threads.

Hot iron transfers were once sold by the Embroiderers' Guild and were very popular. This design is from EG transfer K22, which was taken from an engraved image on the cover of an 18th century copper warming pan. The story of this transfer was described in a 1955 issue of *Embroidery* magazine, which tells of the finding of the warming pan in an antiques shop in Yorkshire. A rubbing was made of the design, which was submitted to the Designs subcommittee at the Embroiderers' Guild for approval. A design was drawn from the rubbing and transfer design K22 was created. It lends itself to many techniques and threads. This piece features felt, beads and surface stitchery in buttonhole, straight and fly stitches.

Maker: D. Britnell
Embroiderers' Guild number: EG1529

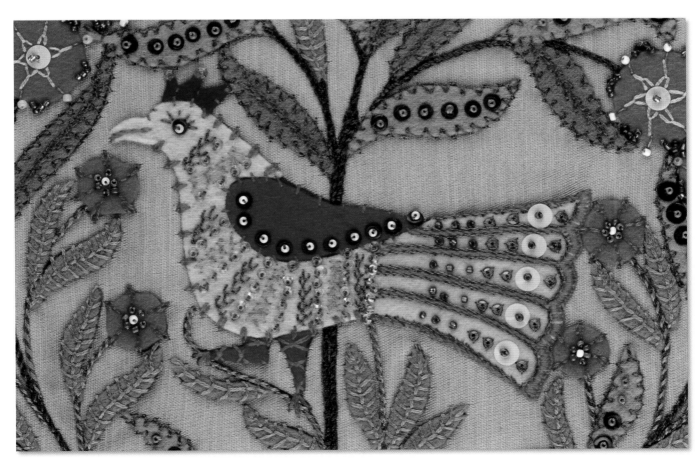

INLAY APPLIQUÉ

TECHNIQUE: inlay appliqué

DATE: 1992

PLACE of origin: Great Britain

SIZE: 34 x 34cm (13½ x 13½in)

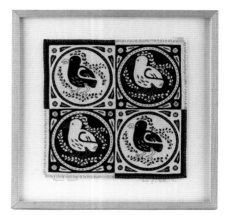

This piece is called 'Birds of a Feather' and the technique used is inlay appliqué. Appliqué as it is usually known is the application of a shape to a base fabric, which is then stitched down with barely visible stitches, or with decorative stitches. In inlay appliqué, two contrasting fabrics are used and the same shape is cut out of each. You then place the piece cut from one fabric into the gap left in the other fabric and stitch it in place. In this example, the fabrics used are black and white felt with surface stitchery in red and white cotton thread. Stitches are straight stitches and single chain stitches. The birds are similar to guinea fowl.

I admire this piece for its technical excellence and design. Compare it to the applied felt bird on page 31. The latter is not an original design, but the technical skill and use of colour have as much impact as in this piece.

Maker: Stephanie Gilbert

Embroiderers' Guild number: EG1992.15

Stephanie is a practising embroiderer and textile artist, based in Norfolk. One of her specialities is inlay appliqué and, more recently, she made an intricate map of the Norfolk coastline using this technique.

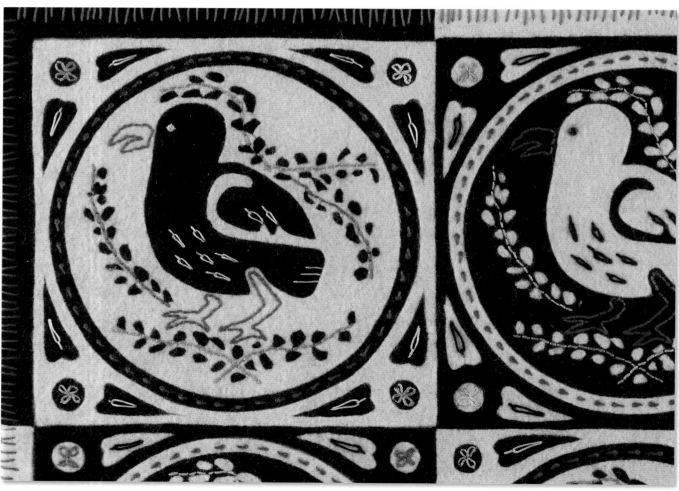

BIRD BY MAIRI McIVER

TECHNIQUE: appliqué
DATE: 1960
PLACE of origin: Great Britain
SIZE: 18 x 17cm (7 x 6¾in)

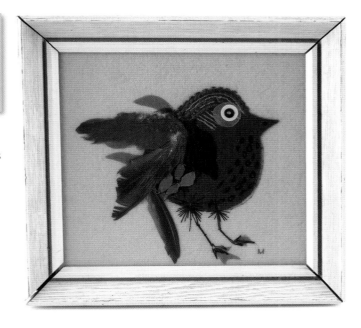

At first glance, this shape of this little blue bird resembles a robin, but with a speckled chest, perhaps it is a thrush. Its title is simply 'Bird'. It is made using felt appliqué on a background of bright yellow felt, with the addition of feathers stitched in place, with three different-sized sequins for the eye.

Surface stitchery is in cotton threads in blue, green, black and brown, using chain stitches and straight stitches. The shadows under the feet are made by using fine net. The design is very simple but effective. Notice how the artist has signed her work in stitch with the letter M.

Maker: Mairi McIver
Embroiderers' Guild number: EG1250

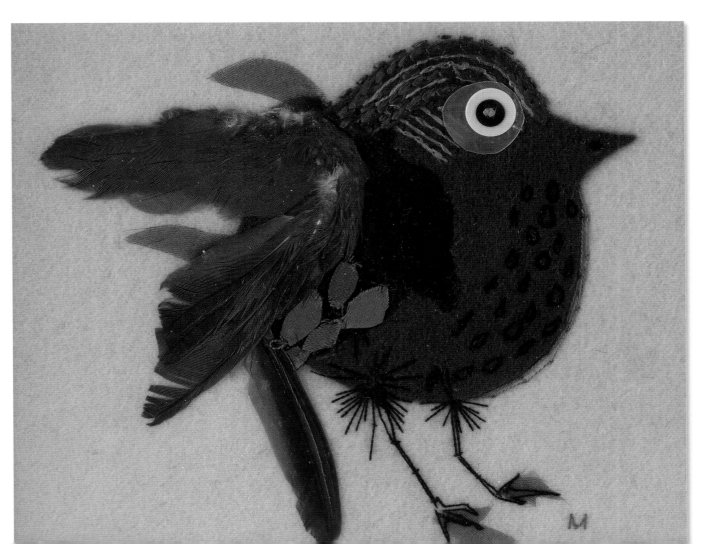

SOLOMON AND SHEBA

TECHNIQUE: hand embroidery

DATE: 1954

PLACE of origin: Great Britain

SIZE: 188 x 41.5cm (74 x 16¼in)

These little birds are a very small part of a long panel with a biblical theme. The Queen of Sheba was a seeker of knowledge and, on hearing that King Solomon of Israel was a very wise man, travelled by camel train to meet him and test his knowledge with difficult questions.

There are four birds visible on this part of the panel, all in felt appliqué using cotton thread; the colour palette is limited and enriched with surface embroidery. Stitches are detached chain stitch, chain stitch and straight stitch. Notice how a star of straight stitches enhances the eyes. One bird is in flight, another is perching on the end of a branch, ready for flight, but I have to say the remaining two birds, to me, resemble flying fishes.

Maker: Winsome Douglass

Gifted by: Needlework Development Scheme

Embroiderers' Guild number: EG1056

The Needlework Development Scheme was an initiative to promote embroidery. Started in 1934 by four Scottish art colleges, it spread south after the Second World War and eventually closed in 1960. Many members of the Embroiderers' Guild were actively involved in the making and collection of embroidery for the Scheme and, after it closed, the Embroiderers' Guild received more than 400 pieces.

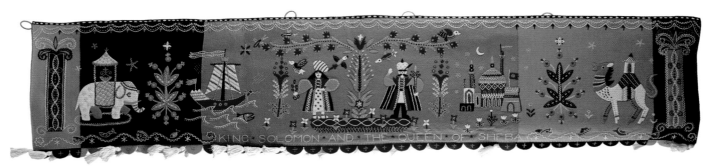

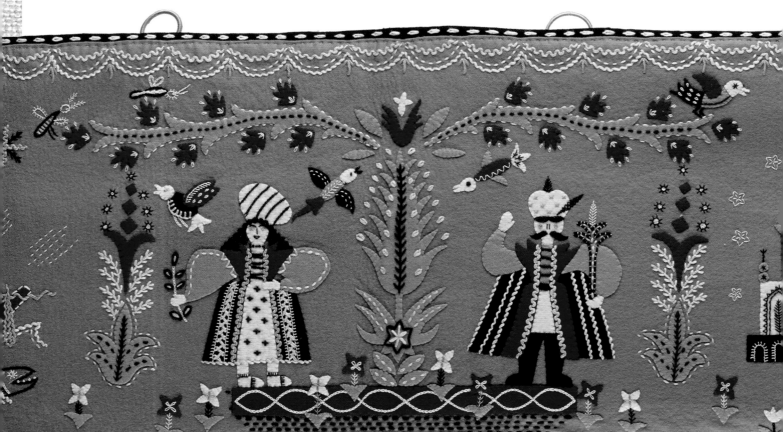

APPLIQUÉ HEN

TECHNIQUE: appliqué
DATE: mid 20th century
PLACE of origin: Great Britain
SIZE: 35 x 34cm (13¾ x 13½in)

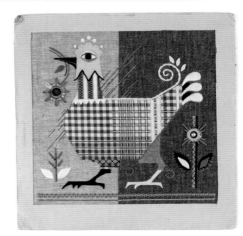

A rather smart hen, sporting a flower in its beak and made from applied gingham and other fabrics, displays surface stitches in cotton thread. Gingham was a very popular fabric for embroidery as the woven squares offered many opportunities for patterns stitched over the squares. Many of us wore school dresses in colourful gingham in those days; my school dresses were red.

Joyce Evans was at Bromley College of Art, where her tutor was Iris Hills, who later moved to Glasgow to head the Needlework Development Scheme, mentioned opposite. The design and stitching of this exercise panel was influenced by the fabrics available. Notice how the dark leg of the bird is contrasted against a lighter background, while the white leg is against a darker background, adding contrast and interest to the design.

Maker: Joyce Evans
Embroiderers' Guild number: EG1772

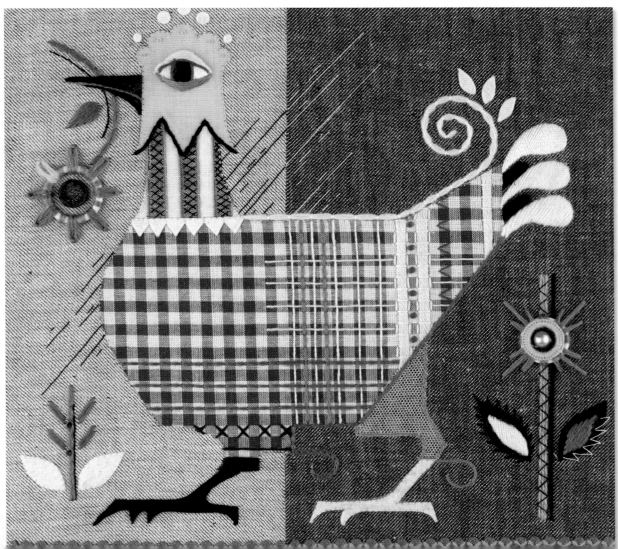

REVERSE APPLIQUÉ MOLA 1

TECHNIQUE: reverse appliqué
DATE: 20th century
PLACE of origin: San Blas Islands (Panama)
SIZE: 45 x 40cm (17¾ x 15¾in)

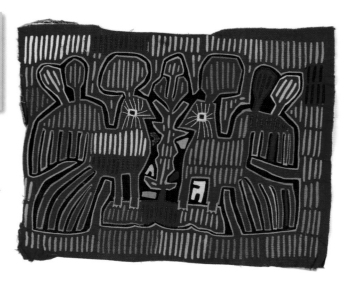

From appliqué, where fabric shapes are applied directly to fabric, and inlaid appliqué where identical shapes are cut from fabric and laid in holes created by the cut shapes, we now turn to reverse appliqué and particularly to the vibrant textiles of the Kuna Indians of the San Blas Islands, off the coast of Panama.

These wonderful designs are molas, traditionally worn as dress panels on the front and back of a blouse. The designs, often of birds or animals, are said to come from ancient face painting designs. Layers of cotton fabric are cut back and the edges turned under and neatly stitched in place to create complex, stylized designs.

For the women of the Kuna Indians, the ability to create a beautifully stitched mola is a source of status.

The colours of this mola and the one on the opposite page are typical of the colours used.

Embroiderers' Guild number: EG1990.33

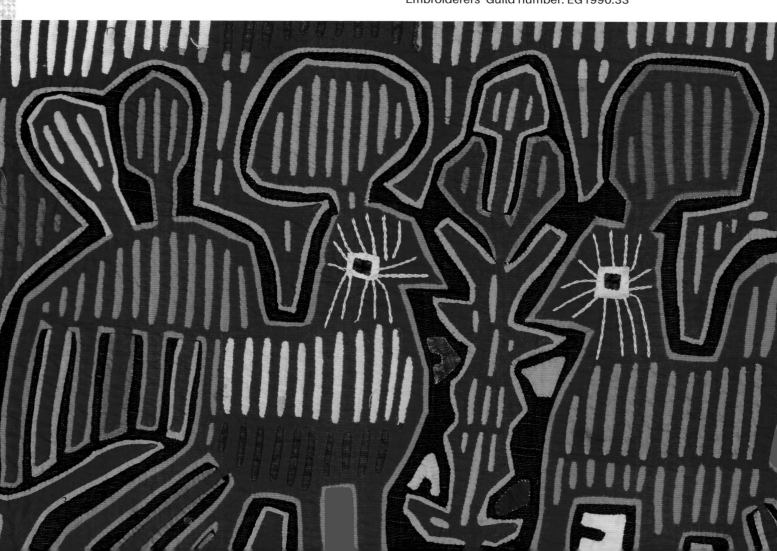

REVERSE APPLIQUÉ MOLA 2

TECHNIQUE: reverse appliqué
DATE: 20th century
PLACE of origin: San Blas Islands (Panama)
SIZE: 45 x 40cm (17¾ x 15¾in)

This is another example of a mola, as described on the opposite page. Molas were often decorated with surface stitches. In these molas, chain stitch lines enhance the eyes. In the mola on this page, cross stitches can be seen beneath the eye. It came to the Embroiderers' Guild Collection as part of a donation from the family of Herta Puls, who was a leading expert on reverse appliqué and was the author of several books on the technique, especially the molas of the Kuna Indians.

Gifted by: the family of Herta Puls
Embroiderers' Guild number: not yet accessioned

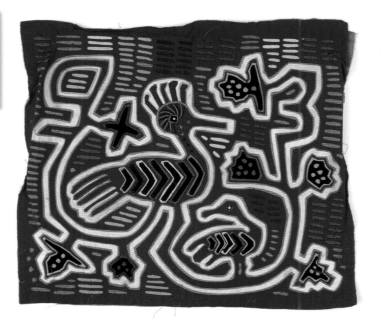

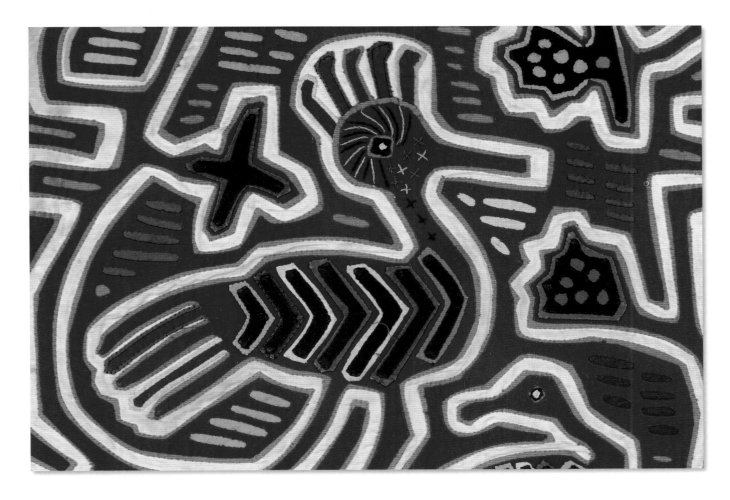

MADE BY
MACHINE

Machine embroidery originated in the 19th century when mill owners were keen to develop methods that would speed up the production of textiles by their workers. In the early 20th century, Dorothy Benson, working for the Singer Sewing Machine Company, became a leading exponent of artistic machine embroidery, followed by others including Joy Clucas. The work of both of these artists is included in this chapter, together with contemporary, free machine embroidery by Jane Poulson, and examples of vermicelli machine embroidery and the use of mixed media with machine embroidery.

Most poignant is a First World War postcard, made on a hand embroidery machine that mimicked hand embroidery so well that it is sometimes not recognized as machine embroidery today.

FIRST WORLD WAR POSTCARD

TECHNIQUE: machine embroidery

DATE: 1916

PLACE of origin: France

SIZE: 14 x 9cm (5½ x 3½in)

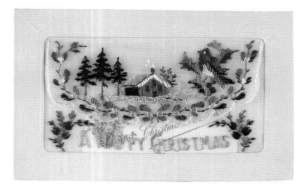

This is a particularly poignant robin on a postcard, produced during the First World War for sale to servicemen, who sent them home to their loved ones. The cards were produced in huge numbers on hand-embroidery machines, which produced multiple cards, mimicking hand embroidery. This card is in the form of an envelope. An insert inside is signed: 'With love, Leslie 18.12.16.'

There is sometimes a misconception that these cards were produced by the servicemen themselves, but with such uniformity of stitch and, given the conditions that servicemen would have worked under, this is very unlikely. It is thought that the original idea came from Belgian nuns, who did stitch some cards by hand. Threads used on the embroidery machines were silk and the finished embroidery was mounted in a card. There were many designs, including this, which wished a Happy Christmas to the recipient. We have a story for this postcard, which was sent to the donor's mother by the donor's uncle, who was serving overseas in the war.

Gifted by: Miss Leslie Page of Carshalton, Surrey.
Embroiderers' Guild number: EG2014.4.7

Perhaps Miss Page was given the masculine form of Lesley as a tribute to her uncle.

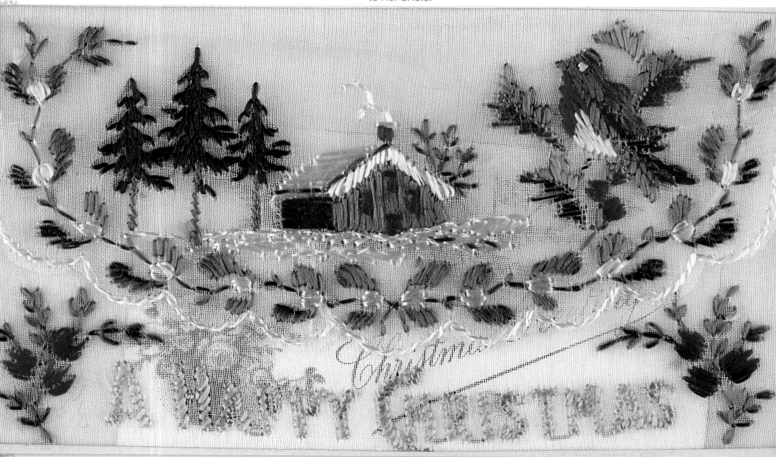

DOROTHY BENSON MAT

TECHNIQUE: machine embroidery
DATE: 1940
PLACE of origin: Great Britain
SIZE: 60cm (23½in) in diameter

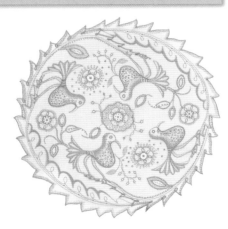

This is an important piece in the Embroiderers' Guild Collection. It is a machine-embroidered mat featuring rather plump birds, and is stitched with silk and aluminium threads on rayon organdie. It was made in the days when sewing machines had no swing needle and computer-operated machines were far in the future.

Dorothy Benson was head of the embroidery department for the Singer Sewing Machine Company at the workshops in London, having joined the company at the age of fourteen. Dorothy was the author of several books on machine embroidery, showing how she achieved her amazing embroideries. She lived in Dorking, Surrey and was a founder member of the Dorking Branch of the Embroiderers' Guild.

After her death, much of her work was given to the branch and branch members gave talks about her work. I have friends who remember Dorothy as a quiet, unassuming branch member, often in charge of the coffee. A few years ago, Dorking Branch relinquished ownership of Dorothy's work and our Collection has several of her best pieces.

Maker: Dorothy Benson
Embroiderers' Guild number: EG2014.106

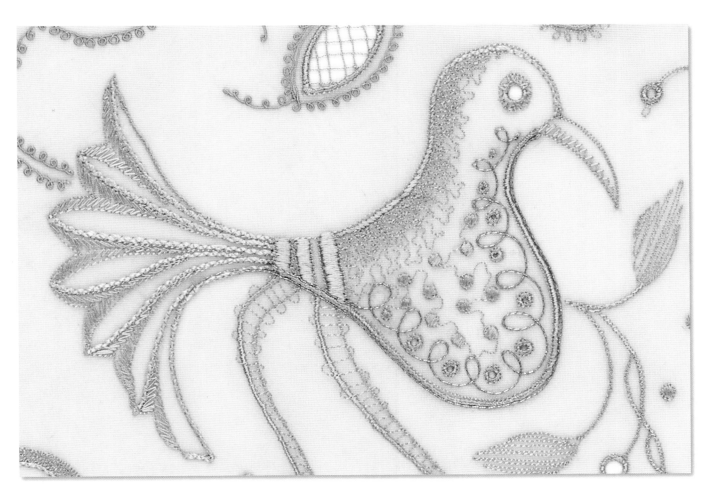

FREE MACHINE EMBROIDERY

TECHNIQUE: machine embroidery

DATE: 1965

PLACE of origin: Great Britain

SIZE: 15 x 26cm (6 x 10¼in)

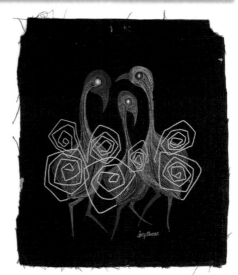

This is my favourite piece in this book. I love the design, as the bird on the right appears to be giving the other two a good telling off.

We have a number of pieces by Joy Clucas in the Collection and all her work is signed in stitch. Reaching her peak later in the 20th century than Dorothy Benson, whose work we looked on the previous page, Joy used free machine embroidery in her work at a time when creative embroidery was coming to the fore. Her sewing machine had a swing needle and the ability to lower the feed dogs on the machine so that the fabric moved freely under the needle while the operator used it as a drawing tool.

Maker: Joy Clucas
Embroiderers' Guild number: EG2016.144

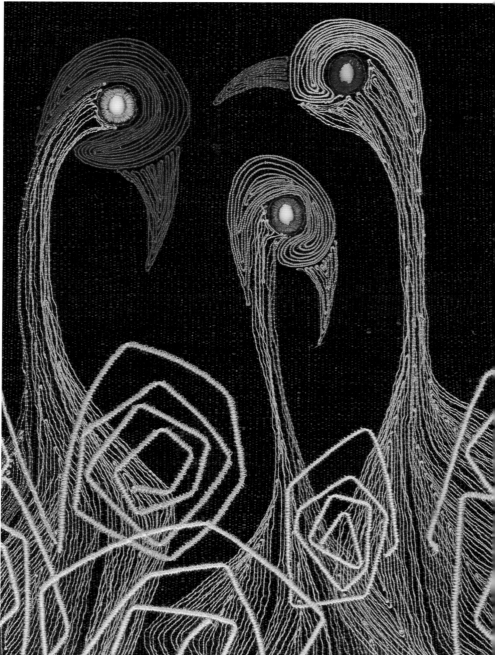

LOOKING BACK

TECHNIQUE: machine embroidery
DATE: 1990
PLACE of origin: Great Britain
SIZE: 30 x 30cm (12 x 12in)

This piece is called 'Looking Back' and is a late 20th century example of free machine embroidery, where the whole surface of the piece is covered in thread. This was purchased from the artist, who trained at Manchester Polytechnic, specializing in embroidery. She is now a well-established textile designer, illustrator and lecturer.

This is an example of Jane's early work. Note how densely this piece is stitched and, in particular, the little heart on the bird's tail, which it is clearly looking at.

Maker: Jane Poulton
Embroiderers' Guild number: EG1991.11

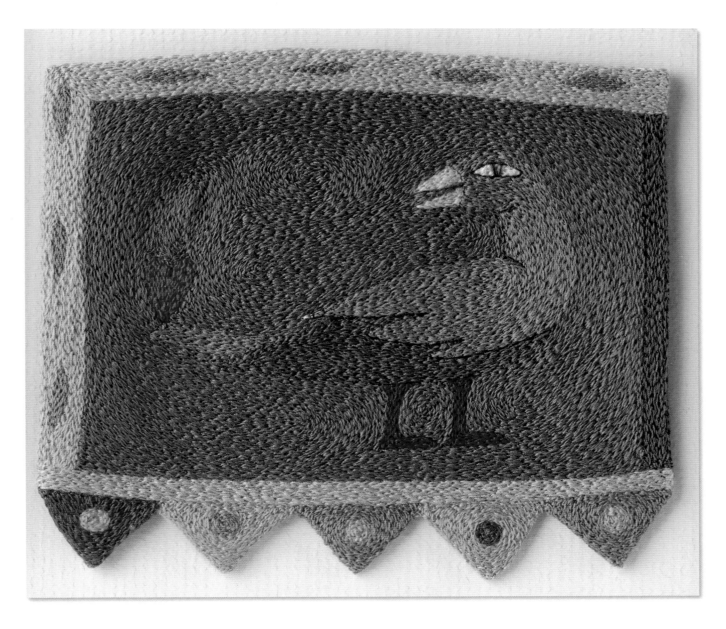

VERMICELLI MACHINE EMBROIDERY

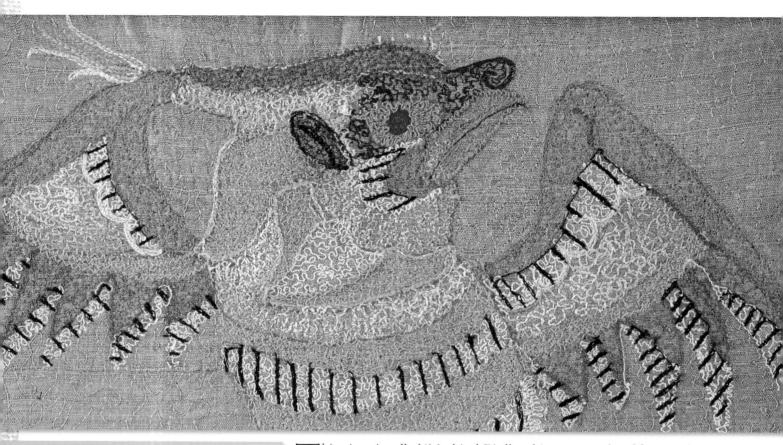

TECHNIQUE: machine embroidery

DATE: 2010

PLACE of origin: Great Britain

SIZE: 30 x 26cm (12 x 10¼in)

This piece is called 'Mythical Bird' and is an example of free machine embroidery using vermicelli stitch where the feed dogs on the machine are lowered so that the fabric can be moved under the free needle, making a continuous meandering line that fills a space, leaving the background fabric showing through. Compare it to the very dense stitching on page 43, where none of the background fabric shows through. Ideally, the fabric should be moved as smoothly as possible so that there are no sudden jerks in the stitched line and lines should not cross each other.

This piece was made for an exhibition by the Woking Evening Branch of the Embroiderers' Guild at Clandon Park in Surrey. Members were allowed to photograph beautiful ceramics in the house and used the photographs as a basis for their embroideries. Very sadly, Clandon Park was destroyed by fire in 2014 and I do not know whether the ceramic bird that inspired this piece survived.

Maker: Annette Collinge

This piece is currently on loan to the Embroiderers' Guild Collection

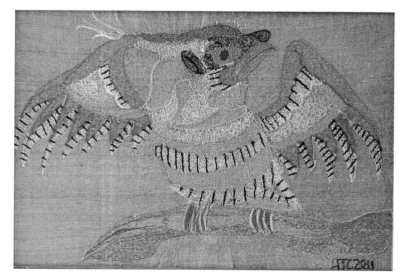

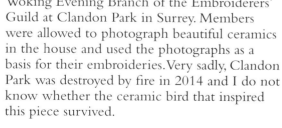

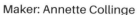

MACHINE EMBROIDERY ON PAPER

TECHNIQUE: mixed media with machine embroidery

DATE: 2010

PLACE of origin: Great Britain

SIZE: 38 x 45cm (15 x 17¾in)

This bird, of no particular species, is made from layers of silk fabrics, cut back to reveal the layers beneath. The background fabric is silk and handmade paper is used in the border.

I make paper myself using old envelopes and unwanted sketch book pages, which I shred, soak and pulp in an old liquidizer. The pulp is added to a large container of water and the paper pulp is caught on a metal mesh, attached to a wooden frame. The paper sheet is rolled from the frame on to a piece of blanket and hung up to dry.

The paper is quite fragile and I used hand embroidery and silk threads to hold it in place. I like to use straight stitches and create shapes with the stitches. Look at the triangle shapes on this bird. I used vermicelli machine embroidery and a little gold synthetic thread. Notice how increasing the density of the meandering line can be used to add shapes within the much less densely stitched background, creating bird shapes. The border is a series of flower and bird designs that merge together.

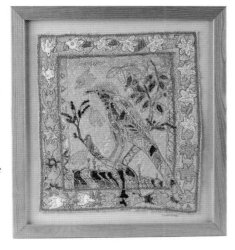

Maker: Annette Collinge

This piece is currently on loan to the Embroiderers' Guild Collection

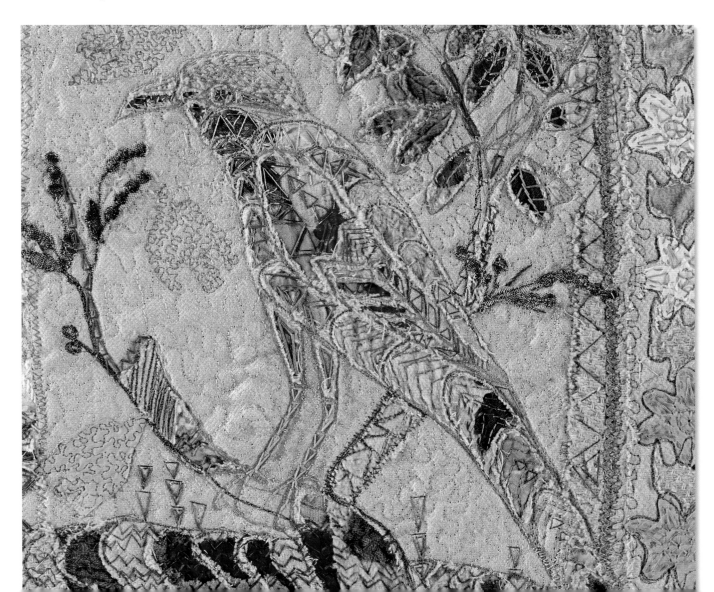

EMBROIDERY
IN SILK

Silk, wool, linen, cotton and synthetics are the most popular fabrics used for embroidery and in this chapter we concentrate on silk, which is ancient in its origins. Spreading from Asia, silk is now universally used and it is arguably at its best in Chinese costume. Most of the examples featuring birds in this chapter are Chinese in origin, but we also look at exquisite embroidery from Japan and an example of tambour work from France.

KIMONO FRAGMENT

TECHNIQUE: silk and metal thread embroidery

DATE: late 19th century

PLACE of origin: Japan

SIZE: 30 x 21cm (12 x 8¼in)

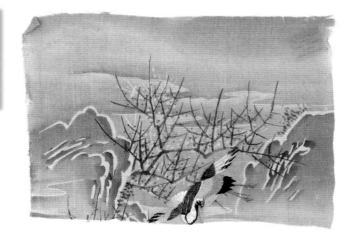

The first four pieces in this chapter come from Japan. This is a costume fragment, probably from a kimono, which is a traditional garment worn by women and men. The kimono can be said to represent the polite and formal in clothing. Kimonos are based on a T-shape, are full length and worn with a wide sash known as an obi. We have a beautiful kimono in the Collection, which we will look at in a later book.

This fragment is silk crepe, onto which is painted or printed a landscape background. Among a shrubby background of twigs and red berries is an embroidered stork in silk thread, some couched metal thread and straight stitches. Whether the stork is taking off or settling on the shrubby twigs is difficult to work out, but its head is bent back and it legs outstretched, which might indicate that it is flying. Note the touches of red and the rather fierce eye, which add contrast to an otherwise subdued colour palette.

Embroiderers' Guild number: EG1982.130.18

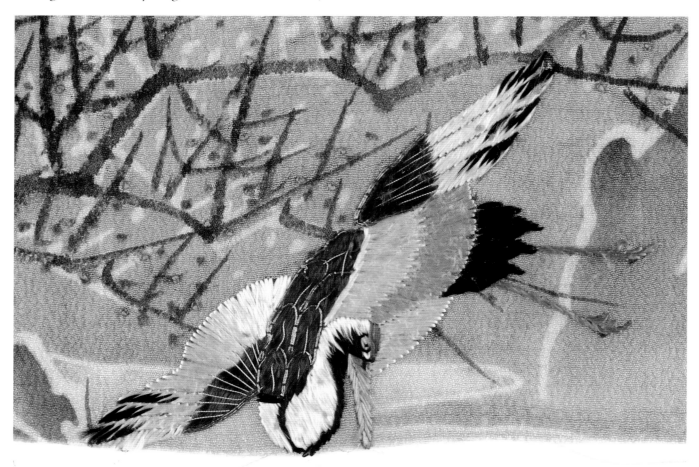

PEACOCK WALL HANGING

TECHNIQUE: silk and metal thread embroidery

DATE: 1907

PLACE of origin: Japan

SIZE: 110.5 x 169cm (43½ x 66½in)

Here is the first of two spectacular hangings from Japan (the second is on page 115). Both are examples of embroideries made for the Western market, during the Meiji period. They were made in the late 19th and early 20th centuries. This hanging can be dated accurately because it has a label attached to the back, which is a rare occurrence.

Two beautiful peacocks are poised on a rock by a stream, surrounded by bamboo and chrysanthemums. The amazing background, on linen fabric, is covered in circles of couched gold thread. Padded satin stitch is found on the peacock's tail feathers and the chrysanthemums. The rocks, stream and bamboo are in satin and long and short stitch, all embroidered in silk threads. No wonder the Western world was enchanted by these textiles.

Embroiderers' Guild number: EG344

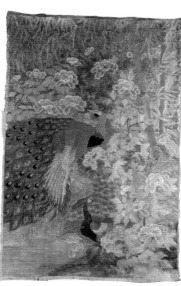

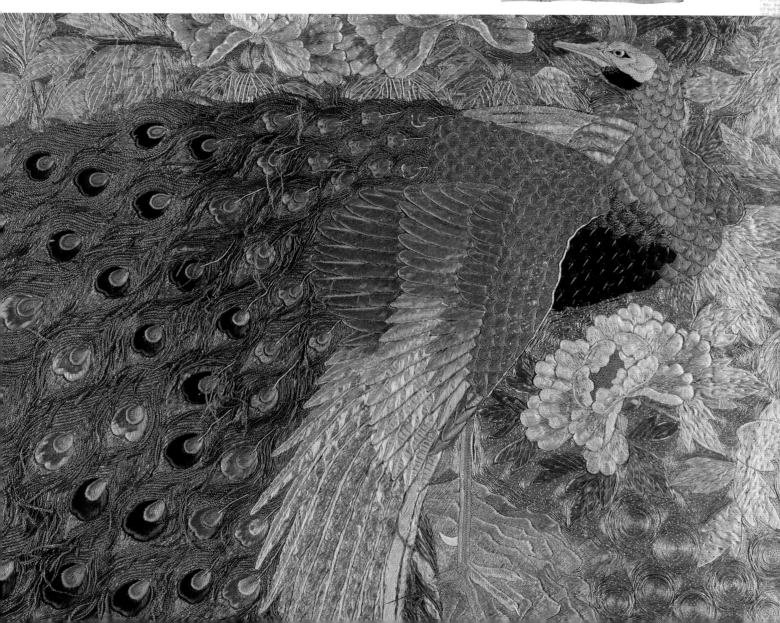

BIRDS WITH CHERRY BLOSSOM

TECHNIQUE: silk embroidery

DATE: late 19th century

PLACE of origin: Japan

SIZE: 39.5 x 45cm (15½ x 17¾in)

This panel is an example of a piece in less-than-perfect condition. The silk background has deteriorated. Silk is particularly vulnerable to light and the fabric was probably red. Rumour has it that it was once ironed onto Vilene, possibly to display it in a frame.

Two delicate little birds are surrounded by branches of white cherry blossom. The threads are floss silk in long and short and satin stitches, and on the bark of the tree is a small area of couched gold threads.

Embroiderers' Guild number: EG2105

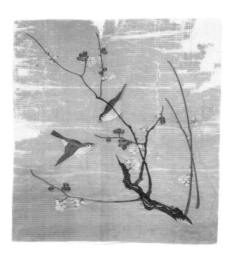

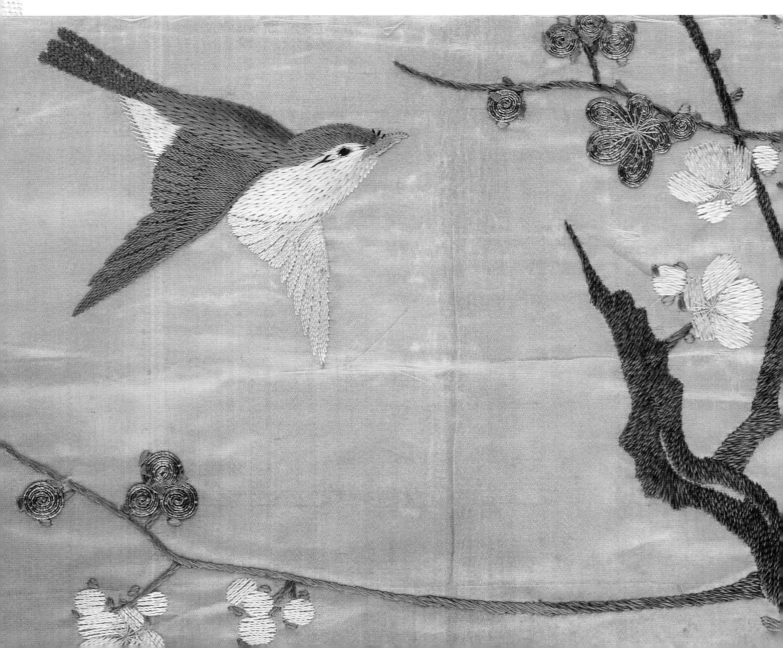

A ROUNDEL OF BIRDS

TECHNIQUE: silk embroidery

DATE: 19th century

PLACE of origin: southeast China (Guangdong)

SIZE: 35.5cm (14in) in diameter

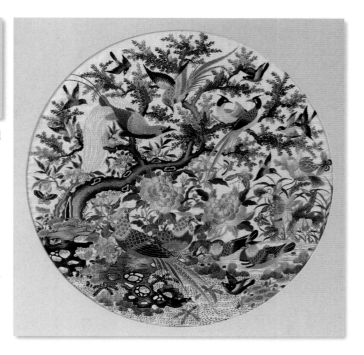

Another of my favourite pieces, this gorgeous roundel of birds, made for export to the Western market, features pairs of birds that are all symbolic. Magpies are birds of joy and mythical, phoenix-like birds called fenghuang only appear in times of prosperity and will only perch on the hardest wood or rest on ground bare of vegetation.

Mandarin ducks symbolize devotion because they mate for life. They are all surrounded by flowers, and peonies in particular. The thread is fine, floss silk in many colours. Stitches are long and short stitch, satin stitch, French knots, stem and backstitches. The background fabric is ivory silk.

Embroiderers' Guild number: EG3899

This was a donation from HM Queen Mary, who was the wife of George V, mother of George VI and patron of the Embroiderers' Guild.

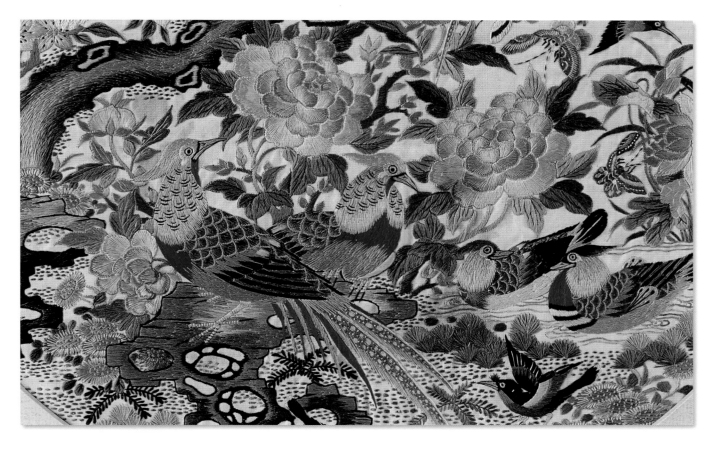

CHINESE SLEEVE BANDS

TECHNIQUE: silk embroidery

DATE: late 19th century

PLACE of origin: China

SIZE: 9 x 92.5cm (3½ x 36½in)

These two bands of embroidery are a pair of sleeve bands from China. They would have been attached to a robe and, if they were a favourite pair, were often unpicked and transferred to other robes.

Here we have a riot of colourful birds: herons standing among tussocks of grass; peacocks perching on a strange blue, flowering branch; and finches, parrots and pheasant-like birds flying and perching among vivid green and blue leaves and purple branches. The fabric is yellow silk damask and the embroidery is in silk thread with straight stitches.

Chinese sleeve bands are beautiful. The background colour is significant as red is the colour of happiness, white is for funerals but yellow, rather like in these sleeve bands, is reserved exclusively for the emperor and empress.

Embroiderers' Guild number: EG3318.1

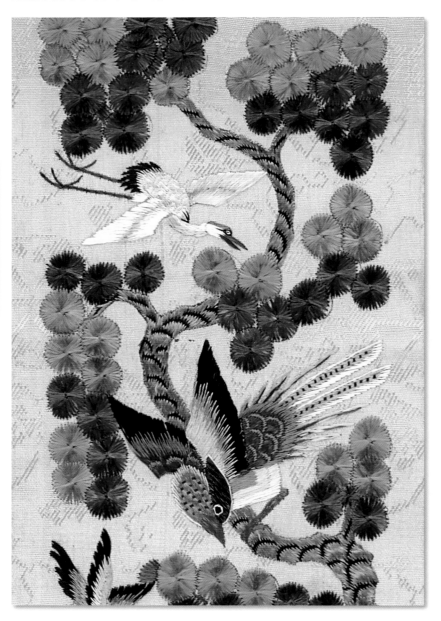

COCKEREL SLEEVE BAND

TECHNIQUE: hand embroidery

DATE: 19th century

PLACE of origin: Great Britain

SIZE: 114.5 x 10cm (45 x 4in)

This is another sleeve band, which would have been one of a pair. Two cockerels are confronting each other, one on a branch looking down on another, which is standing on the ground. To me, they look more surprised than angry. They are surrounded by flowers, butterflies and other birds, but in this sleeve band, the cockerels take centre stage.

The background is cream satin and the threads are silk. The embroidery is similar to the pair of sleeve bands opposite, but the colours are less vibrant and the design is less exuberant, with most of the embroidery receding into the background, bringing the two cockerels to the fore.

Embroiderers' Guild number: EG347

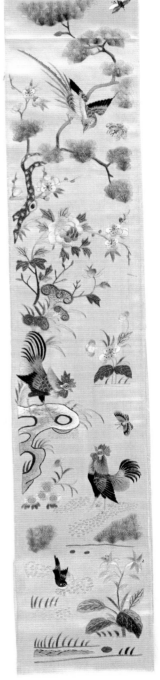

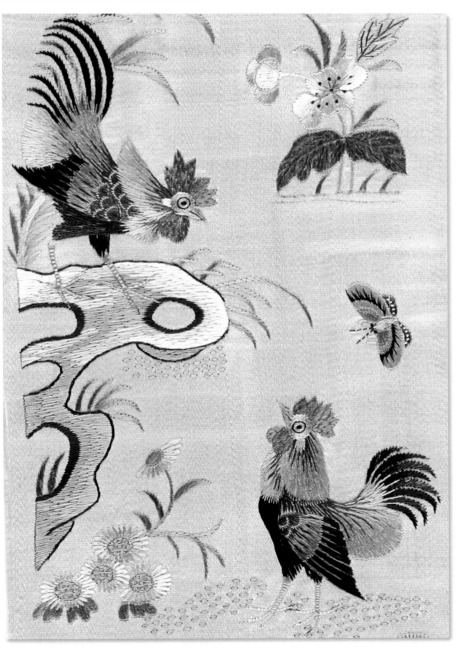

MIRROR IMAGE SLEEVE BAND

TECHNIQUE: silk embroidery

DATE: early 20th century

PLACE of origin: China

SIZE: 35.5 x 109.5cm (14 x 43in)

This panel on pink satin with silk threads and embroidered with straight stitches could be divided to make two sleeve bands. The designs on either side are mirror images of each other. This panel is catalogued as early 20th century.

The embroidery is less fine than in the sleeve bands seen earlier, which is an indication of more recent embroideries and this piece might have been made for the Western market. The design is the now familiar one of birds, insects and flowers among leafy branches.

Embroiderers' Guild number: EG4298

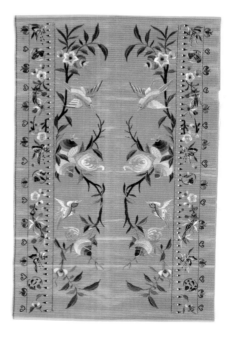

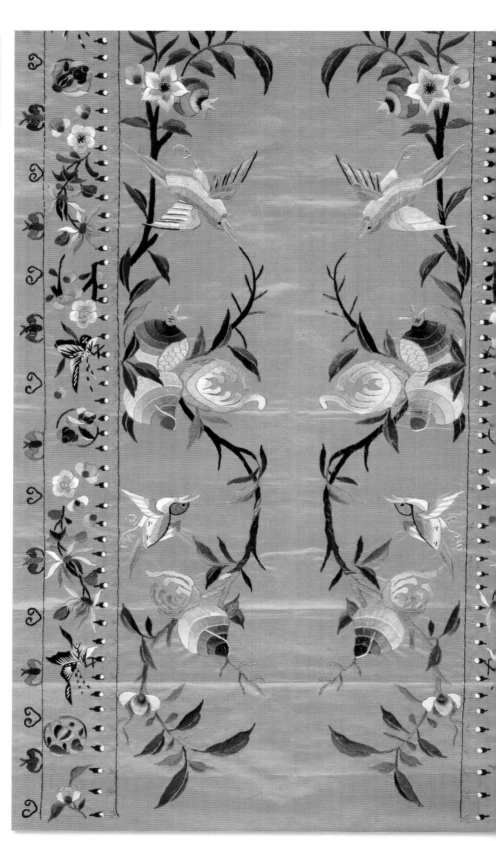

FENGHUANG BIRDS PANEL

TECHNIQUE: silk embroidery

DATE: early 19th century

PLACE of origin: China

SIZE: 38 x 27cm (15 x 10½in)

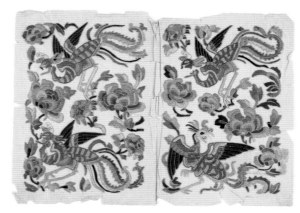

We saw examples of these birds on the roundel or circular embroidery on page 51. They are described as fenghuang – phoenix-like birds that appear in times of prosperity. In the roundel, they are much more realistic than these stylized versions.

All the motifs on this embroidery have been stitched onto paper. They would have been cut out, close to the embroidery, and applied to fabric. Silk threads have been used and the stitches are satin stitch, with some couched metal thread and Pekin knots. These tiny knots have become known as the forbidden stitch, believed to be because workers became blind after hours of stitching. A more likely explanation is that the stitch was practised in the Forbidden City – the Chinese Imperial Palace from 1420–1920 – which is in central Beijing.

There are two panels of the same designs, but look closely at them and you will see variations in colour and stitching; a sure indication that these motifs are hand embroidered, rather than made on a machine.

Embroiderers' Guild number: EG4224

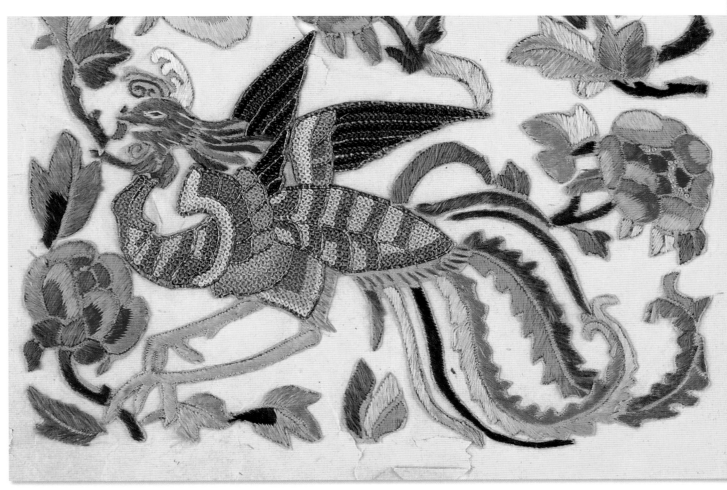

SHOES FOR BOUND FEET

TECHNIQUE: silk embroidery, shoes for bound feet
DATE: early 19th century
PLACE of origin: China
SIZE: length of sole: 7cm (2¾in)

Both beautiful and repellent, these little birds are embroidered in silk thread and straight stitches on a pair of shoes for bound feet. The practice of binding feet is thought to have originated from a tribal custom, to prevent women straying far from home.

It became widespread and it was not until 1911 that a law was passed forbidding the custom, which was deforming and crippling. It conferred status, as peasant women could not afford to bind feet. Binding started at the age of three or four and bandages were never completely removed. The practice was considered to enhance femininity and was associated with female delicacy. It reinforced the status of men, as the women needed support to walk and were conveyed in sedan chairs if any distance was to be covered. Notice how the soles of the shoes were embroidered, too (see below left). This was because the soles would be visible when the wearer sat cross-legged.

Embroiderers' Guild number: EG1987.7

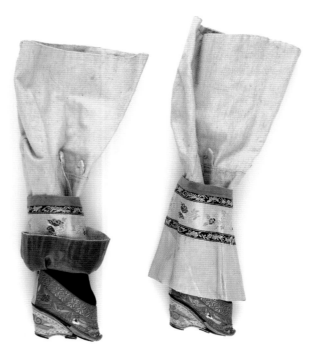

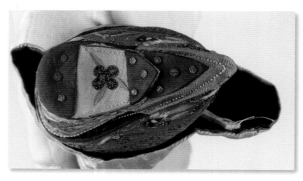

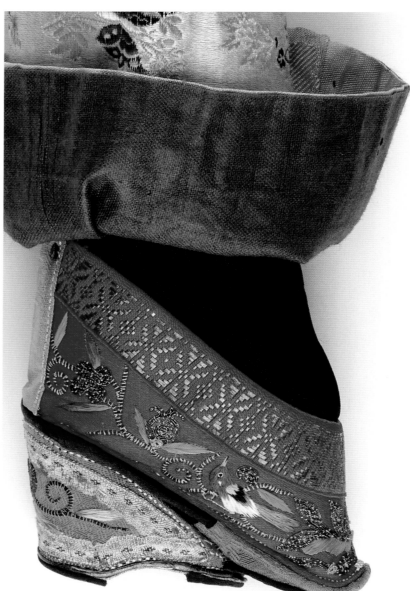

TAMBOUR WORK PANEL

TECHNIQUE: silk embroidery, tambour work
DATE: 1780
PLACE of origin: France
SIZE: 55 x 49.5cm (21½ x 19½in)

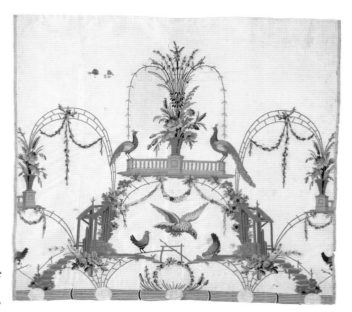

This dress panel was one of the earliest pieces in the Collection to be catalogued when the catalogue was transferred to the computer. It is French and probably the central panel of a dress. Notice the differences in design between this Western style of embroidery and that of the Eastern embroideries in this chapter. There is no symbolism here and the garden scenes are realistic. There are peacocks, chickens and other birds in an exotic garden featuring ironwork and stone.

The background is ivory silk and the threads are silk. The technique is tambour embroidery. Tambour is French for drum, which refers to the fact that the fabric is very tightly stretched. A tambour hook is used to create a chain stitch. The fabric is stretched on a frame and the hook catches the thread from the back, making the chain stitches.

Embroiderers' Guild number: EG7b

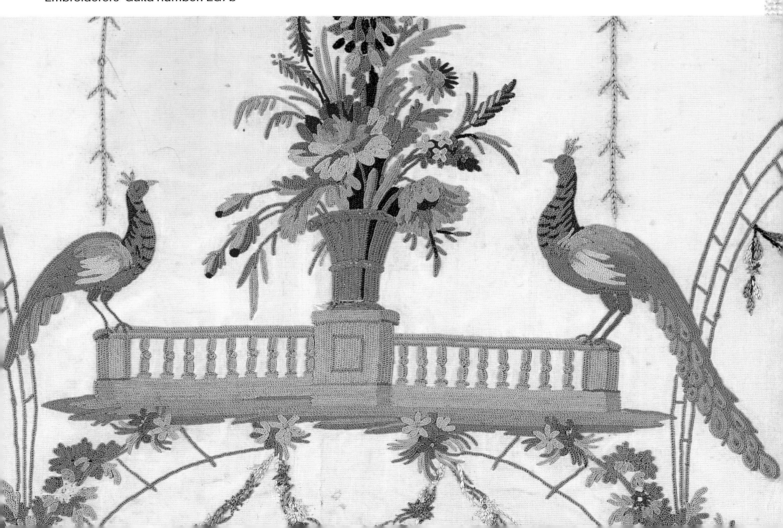

EMBROIDERY ON
EVENWEAVE BACKGROUNDS

An evenweave background can be anything from delicate muslin through to a coarse canvas and includes net. In most cases, the embroidery is executed by counting threads in the ground fabric. In some cases, threads are withdrawn and cut from the fabric, as seen in the pulled thread parrots in this chapter. There are many examples of counted thread birds in this book. This chapter features birds executed in cross stitch and a 17th century beadwork panel.

PULLED THREAD PARROTS

TECHNIQUE: pulled thread
DATE: 20th century
PLACE of origin: Great Britain
SIZE: 51 x 46cm (20 x 18in)

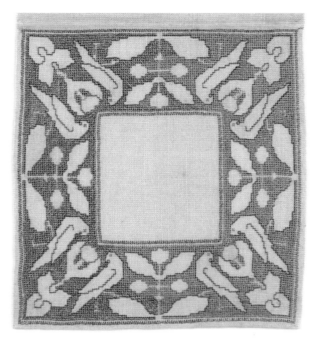

The evenweave linen fabric of this cloth makes it ideal for counted thread work. The pairs of parrots on either side of a stylized flower are shown in outline with straight stitches outlining the wings and feet. The wide border is pulled thread work where threads have been withdrawn and cut away from the fabric, leaving the remaining threads as a mesh. This is then overworked with thread, making a dense background. In this example, linen threads have been used in red and black.

Embroiderers' Guild number: not yet accessioned

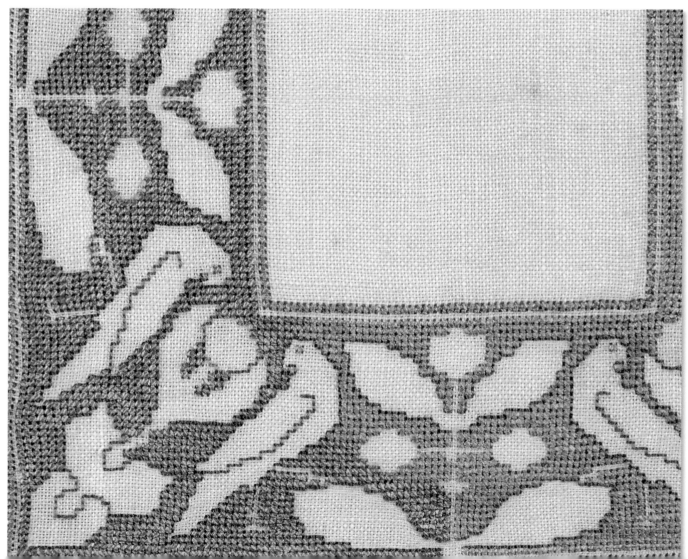

CROSS STITCH PEACOCK

TECHNIQUE: canvas work

DATE: mid 20th century

PLACE of origin: Great Britain

SIZE: 32 x 21.5cm (12½ x 8½in)

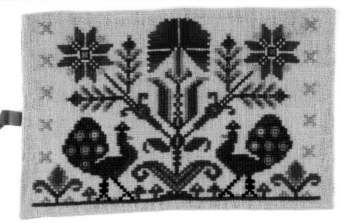

This piece appeals to me for its bright colours, symmetrical design and beautifully executed embroidery. The background is canvas and the threads used are wool. It is worked in cross stitch and the design is clearly of peacocks. This is one of a number of samples in the Collection made by Phyllis Farwell.

Mrs Farwell, from West Sussex, was a member of the Embroiderers' Guild and a teacher. This piece is thought to be one of her teaching samples. It is the only pictorial sample among a series of geometrical samples. All the samples came to the Guild as a donation from Mrs M. Halligan in 1984. Mrs Halligan had been given the samples by the maker several years before her death. This is how many pieces in our Collection reach us; passed from maker to family member or friend and eventually to the Collection.

Maker: Phyllis Farwell
Gifted by: Mrs M. Halligan
Embroiderers' Guild number: EG1984.58.4

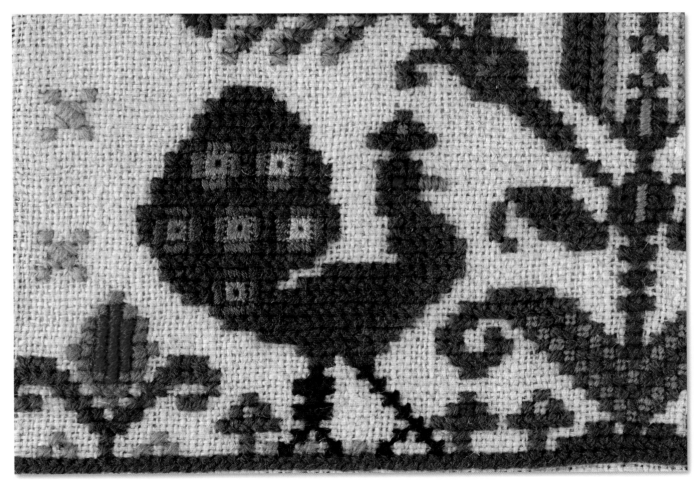

CROSS STITCH PANELS

TECHNIQUE: canvas work

DATE: late 20th century

PLACE of origin: Sweden

SIZE: 17 x 17cm (6¾ x 6¾in)

Two of these four birds are instantly recognizable as a blue tit and a green woodpecker (top left and bottom left). I am not so sure of the other two. The bird on the top right may be a waxwing and the bird on the bottom right could be a redstart. Like the peacock on the opposite page, these were purchased through an internet auction site and are typical of 20th century domestic embroideries from Sweden. They are cross stitch on canvas using wool threads in the natural colours of the birds depicted.

Embroiderers' Guild number: EG2015.23

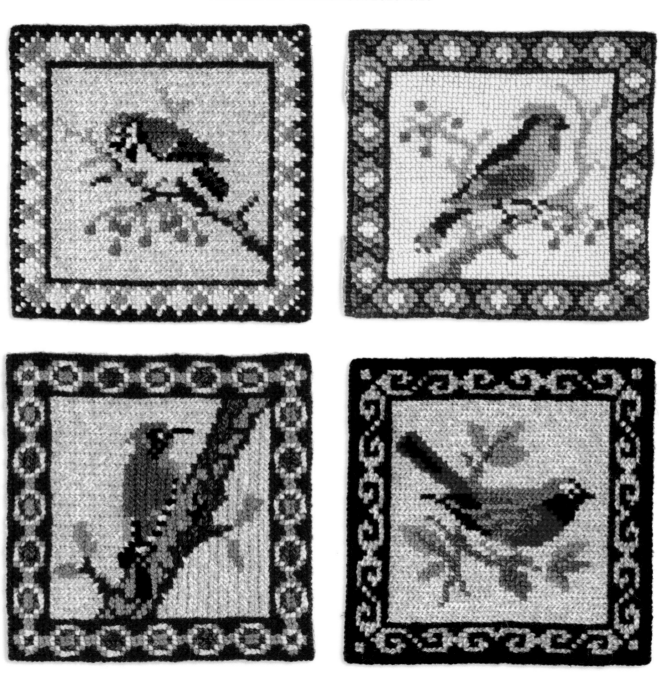

CANVAS WORK PEACOCK

TECHNIQUE: canvas work

DATE: late 20th century

PLACE of origin: Sweden

SIZE: 27 x 27cm (10½ x 10½in)

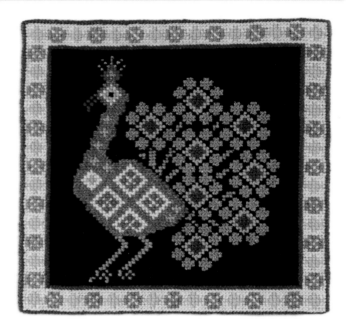

This example of cross stitch in wool threads on a canvas background is a peacock; a lovely design that could easily be copied, perhaps with variations in colour and even using threads other than wool.

There are areas in the Collection where we do not have many examples, or perhaps the examples we have represent a particular technique. This means there is not always a full picture of the textiles of the area concerned. Scandinavia is one such area, where we have many examples of whitework. But this piece and the birds on the opposite page represent embroideries found today in Swedish homes. They were purchased on an internet auction site from Anitha Jacquemont, who is herself Swedish.

Embroiderers' Guild number: EG2015.22

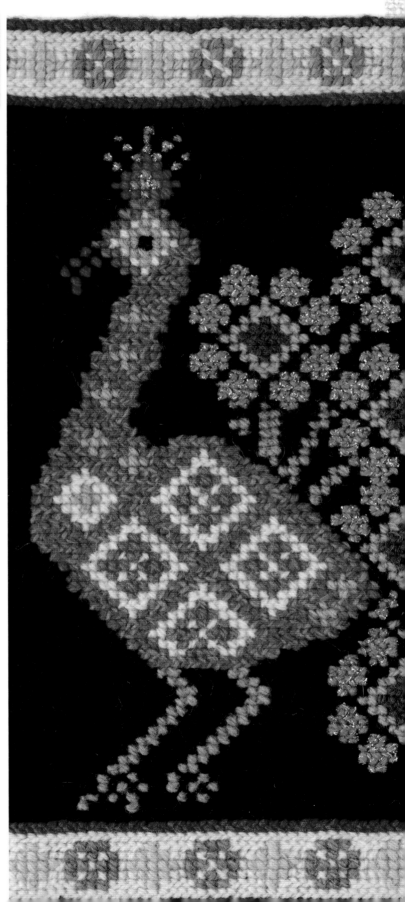

CROSS STITCH BAG

TECHNIQUE: cross stitch
DATE: 19th century
PLACE of origin: Italy
SIZE: 43 x 36.5cm (17 x 14½in)

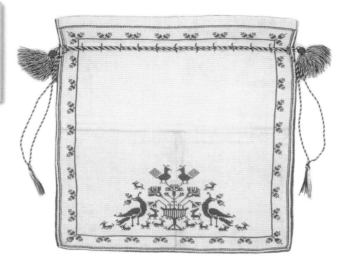

This is a drawstring bag from Italy in cross stitch on natural linen fabric. The threads are linen and this is a monochrome piece where the same brown thread has been used throughout the design.

The bag is embroidered on one side only. The design has a border of flower sprigs. Two peacocks are facing away from each other, with what appear to be flowers in their beaks. There is an interesting example of scale here as there is a flock of tiny deer at the feet and above the heads of the peacocks.

Embroiderers' Guild number: EG1993

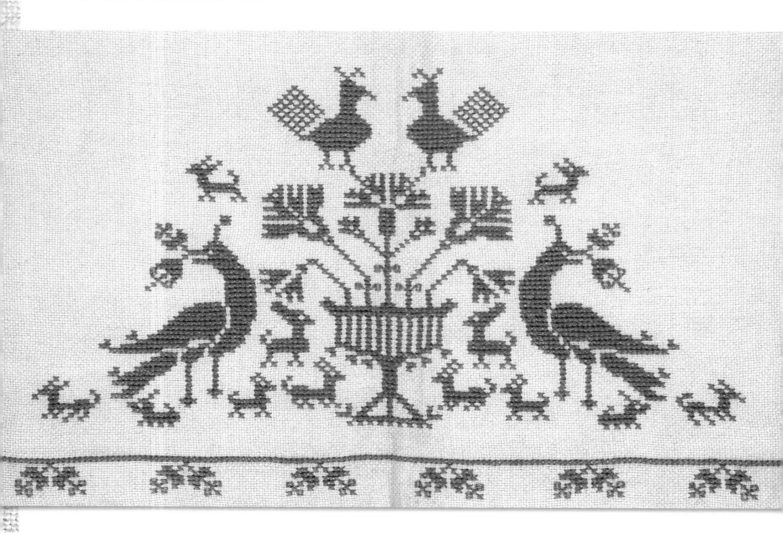

BEADWORK PANEL

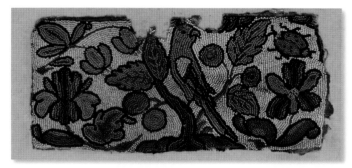

TECHNIQUE: beadwork

DATE: 17th century

PLACE of origin: Great Britain

SIZE: 25 x 11cm (10 x 4¼in)

This bird, looking very much like a parrot, is part of three beaded panels, thought to be the top and two sides of a box which might contain an Elizabethan gentleman's ruff or collar.

The original fabric is linen but these panels have been glued on to cardboard quite recently. This has prevented bead loss and the beads, which are made of glass, have retained their lustre. The fabric is entirely covered with beads, which are stitched in place using linen thread. The colourful parrot perches on a leafy branch against a background of white beads.

We have no provenance for this piece but we do know it was part of the Collection before 1987. The 'T' in the catalogue number stands for 'temporary', which remains until the piece is accessioned permanently into the Collection, when it is given an EG number. I am intrigued as to why the box was never finished.

Embroiderers' Guild number: T329

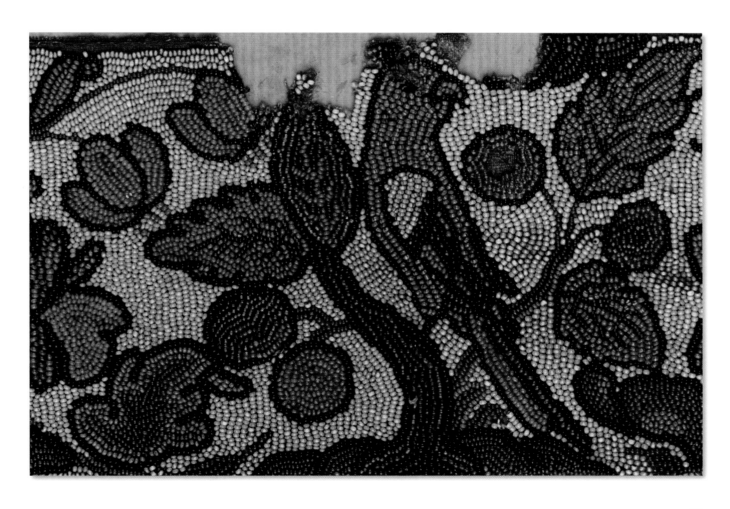

EMBROIDERY
ON BAGS

There are many bags in the Embroiderers' Guild Collection with a wide range of techniques and styles from counted thread to crochet, evening bags to bridal bags, beading to quilting and miser's purses to tobacco pouches.

In this chapter, we look at a tiny selection of bags, all featuring birds.

Some have an interesting provenance, such as the beautifully quilted bag from the School of Needlework and Lace in Surrey, and the bag made by a totally disabled serviceman after the First World War. Other bags leave their provenance to the imagination of the reader.

SILK WITH METAL THREAD

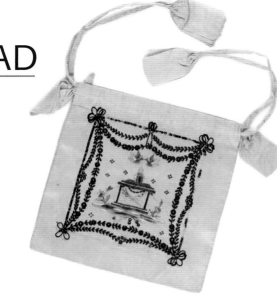

TECHNIQUE: silk embroidery with metal thread

DATE: 18th century

PLACE of origin: France

SIZE: 24 x 24cm (9½ x 9½in)

Our first bag is from France. Compare it to the dress panel seen on page 57 and notice similarities in design: the way the birds are stitched and floral swags in silk thread on the dress panel and metal thread on the bag.

The bag is cream satin and the embroidery in silk thread, with couched metal purls, sequins, or spangles and paste jewels, which are held in place by circles of couched metal purl. Purl thread, which is like a coiled spring, was often used to hold spangles in place, as the needle could be passed through the length of purl, the hole in the spangle and the fabric. The flowers in the swag above the birds have been stitched in this way.

This bag speaks of love. The two birds are kissing and beneath them is an altar to love with two entwined and flaming hearts. Beneath is a chain and Cupid's bow with quiver of arrows, crossed with a flaming torch.

Embroiderers' Guild number: EG3839

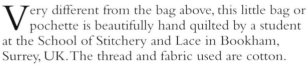

QUILTING

TECHNIQUE: quilting

DATE: mid 20th century

PLACE of origin: Great Britain (School of Stitchery and Lace)

SIZE: 15.5 x 15.5cm (6 x 6in)

Very different from the bag above, this little bag or pochette is beautifully hand quilted by a student at the School of Stitchery and Lace in Bookham, Surrey, UK. The thread and fabric used are cotton.

The School started life in Leicestershire, before moving to Bookham in 1938 as the Grange Centre for Disabled People. It offered a three-year course in needlework.

Now called The Grange Centre, it is a centre of excellence in crafts and horticulture, admitting both men and women. The charity still provides opportunities for disabled adults. Sadly we do not have a name for the maker of this lovely piece, but the quality of the workmanship speaks for itself.

Embroiderers' Guild number: EG972

Reverse of bag

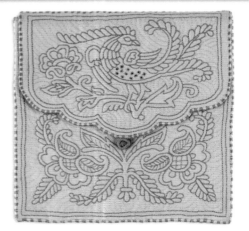

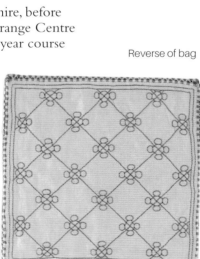

CANVAS WORK

TECHNIQUE: petit point canvas work
DATE: 20th century
PLACE of origin: Great Britain
SIZE: 13 x 17cm (5 x 6¾in)

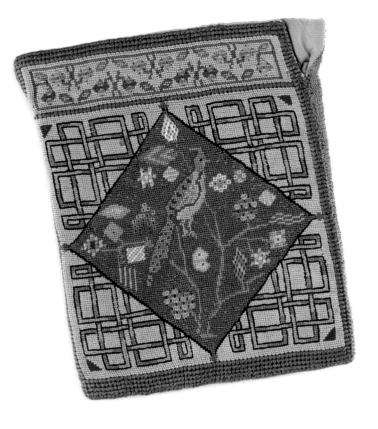

This bag is an example of fine canvas work embroidery or petit point, in silk thread. The bird, which is a peacock, perches rather formally on flowering branches within a diamond shape, against a background of a geometric strap design. Beneath it is a butterfly. The back of the bag is covered in panels of geometric designs.

Unfortunately we have no provenance for this lovely, colourful bag and can only speculate on the source of the design.

The bag is worked mainly in tent stitch, but look at the stitches within the diamond and you will find areas of canvas work stitches, including cross stitch, straight stitches and eyelets.

Embroiderers' Guild number: EG1444

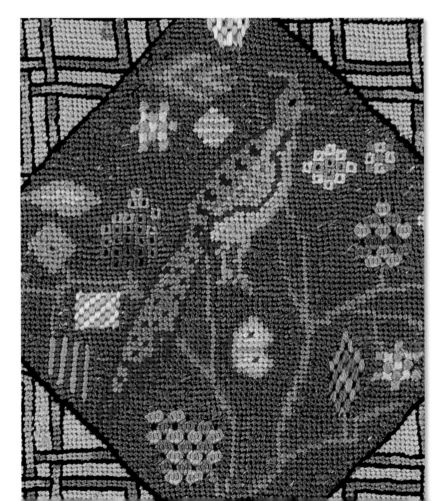

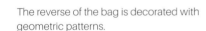
The reverse of the bag is decorated with geometric patterns.

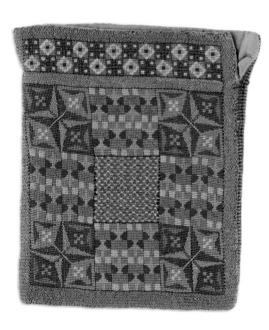

PETIT POINT CANVAS WORK

TECHNIQUE: petit point canvas work
DATE: 1951
PLACE of origin: England
SIZE: 24.5 x 43cm (9¾ x 17in)

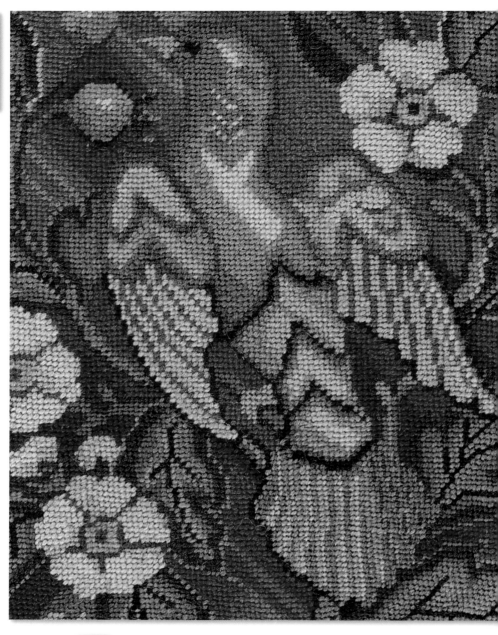

A spectacular example of fine canvas work embroidery or petit point, this is worked using wool thread. It is stitched in tent stitch. This bird is clearly sunning himself, wings and tail outstretched, surrounded by flowers and leaves.

In this example, the back of the bag is particularly interesting. Beneath a rose are the initials JHD and the date, 1951. I always feel a sense of satisfaction to find a beautiful embroidery in any form, where the artist has been proud of her achievement and has signed her work.

This bag was designed and worked for an exhibition by the Women's Institute (WI). Joan Drew was an active member of the WI in Surrey and, during and after the First World War, she and her students designed and made a series of banners for Blackheath village hall. She was a lecturer, teacher and excellent exponent of embroidery. The Embroiderers' Guild is lucky enough to own three of her banners.

Maker: Joan H. Drew
Gifted by: Kathleen Aldworth, niece of Joan Drew
Embroiderers' Guild number: EG1999.25

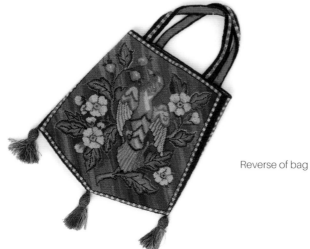

Front of bag

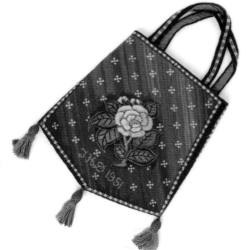

Reverse of bag

SOLDIERS EMBROIDERY INDUSTRY

TECHNIQUE: hand embroidery
DATE: 1914–1918
PLACE of origin: England
SIZE: 8 x 8cm (3¼ x 3¼in)

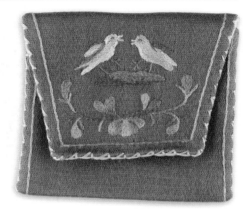

This little purse has a poignant story to tell. It is made of cotton sateen fabric and stitched in split stitch using cotton thread. There are two little birds back and front, clearly chatting to each other.

Inside the purse is the characteristic label of the Soldiers Embroidery Industry of 42 Ebury Street, London, which states that it was 'made by the totally disabled' (see below right). This organization was active during and after the First World War to provide work for disabled servicemen. Much of the work was domestic, but it also included large-scale projects for churches and civic buildings. The Embroiderers' Guild holds the largest collection of work from the Soldiers Embroidery Industry in the country, including a Union Jack pincushion and this little purse.

Maker: Soldiers Embroidery Industry, London
Embroiderers' Guild number: EG1999.31

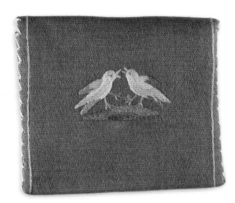

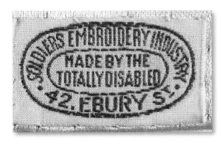

The reverse of the purse (left) also features two little birds.

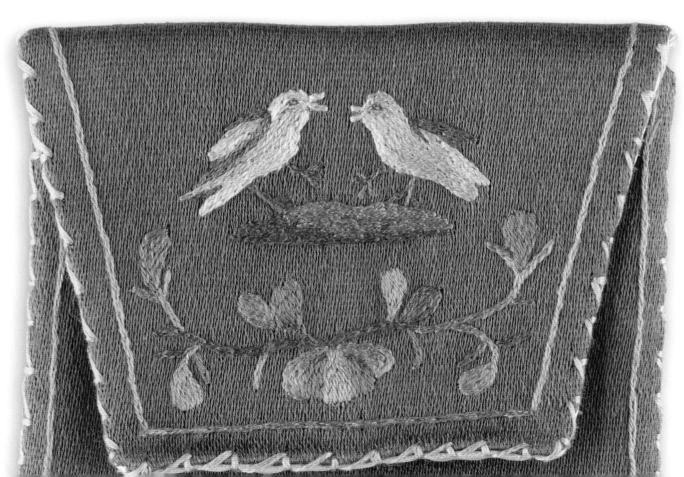

FABRIC APPLIQUÉ BAG

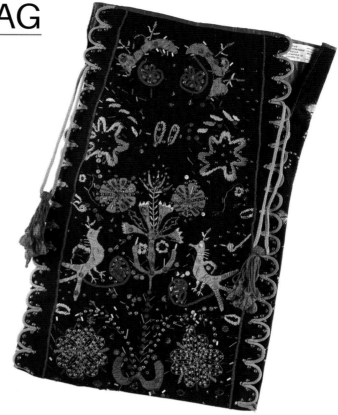

TECHNIQUE: Fabric appliqué
DATE: 19th century
PLACE of origin: Spain
SIZE: 36.5 x 57.5cm (14¼ x 22¾in)

This large bag, described as a bridal bag, is of black woollen fabric embellished with applied fabrics, sequins, couched cord and chenille thread with a little silk thread. The birds are stylized with sequins for eyes and satin stitch for their legs. This cannot be described as fine embroidery, but has immediacy about it and is a lovely example of folk embroidery.

Gifted by: Mrs Harkness, who gave several embroideries from Spain to the Collection
Embroiderers' Guild number: EG67

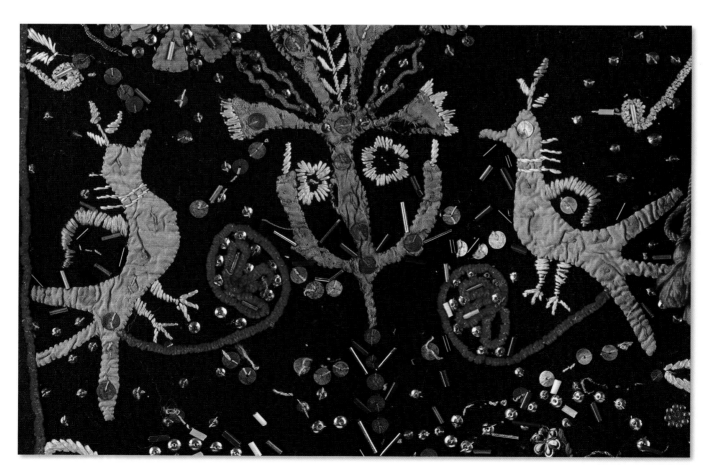

METAL THREAD BEADWORK

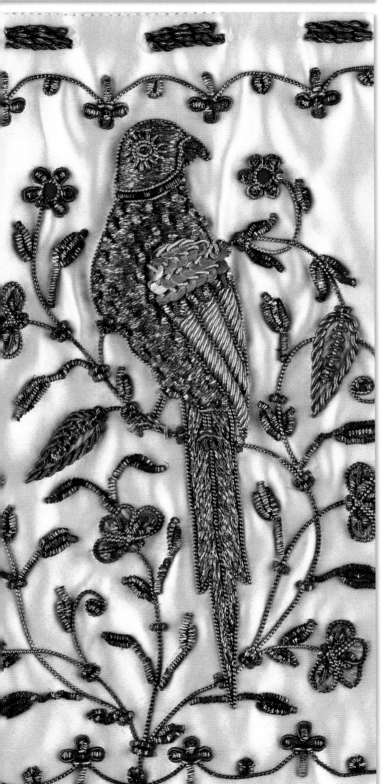

TECHNIQUE: metal thread, beadwork

DATE: unknown

PLACE of origin: unknown, but possibly India

SIZE: 17 x 16cm (6¾ x 6¼in)

Although no date or place is recorded for this little satin bag with a parrot surrounded by flowers, it is very Indian in style and the techniques of padded areas covered with beads, couched metal thread and sequins should be compared to the Indian peacocks we saw in Chapter 2. The flowers in particular are very similar.

Notice how the parrot is looking backwards and compare it with Jane Poulton's 'Looking Back' on page 43. In that example, the bird looks backwards towards a heart on its tail and here, the parrot is looking backwards at a flower.

Gifted by: Hester Clough
Embroiderers' Guild number: EG1987.43

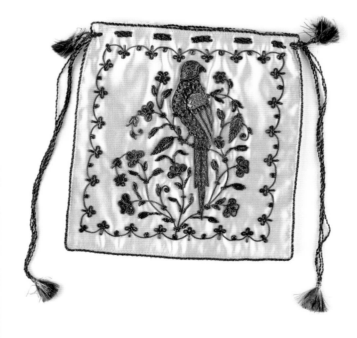

BIRDS
AS ART

There is a long-standing argument among embroiderers and craftspeople as to what makes an embroidery 'art' as opposed to 'craft'. In my opinion, a beautiful embroidery showing excellence of technique is as valid an art form as work that is perceived to be textile art.

In this chapter, I have tried to demonstrate this by including embroideries that encompass both categories. Some work is by recognized contemporary textile artists and undoubtedly qualifies as art, with original designs and use of fabric and threads, while others are excellent examples of recognized techniques from the 19th and 20th centuries.

THE OWL ON A BRANCH

TECHNIQUE: fabric appliqué

DATE: 1950s

PLACE of origin: England

SIZE: 58 x 43cm (23 x 17in)

We have a total contrast in style at the beginning of this chapter. This is free appliqué work using furnishing fabrics, slubbed velvet, tweed and knitted jersey with various thick and thin threads. Look how this free approach to appliqué creates movement in the owl and its feathers. Compare it to the rigid bird shapes on the Spanish bridal bag in the previous chapter and other examples of appliqué in earlier chapters. The artist of this piece was interested in textural and tonal values and the effects of light created by her chosen fabrics.

'The Owl on a Branch' was purchased for the Embroiderers' Guild Collection by the East Sussex branch.

Maker: Margaret Kaye
Embroiderers' Guild number: EG1983.106

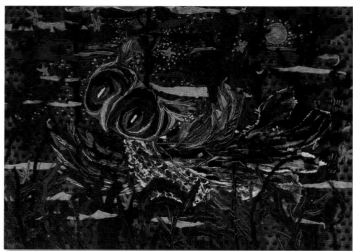

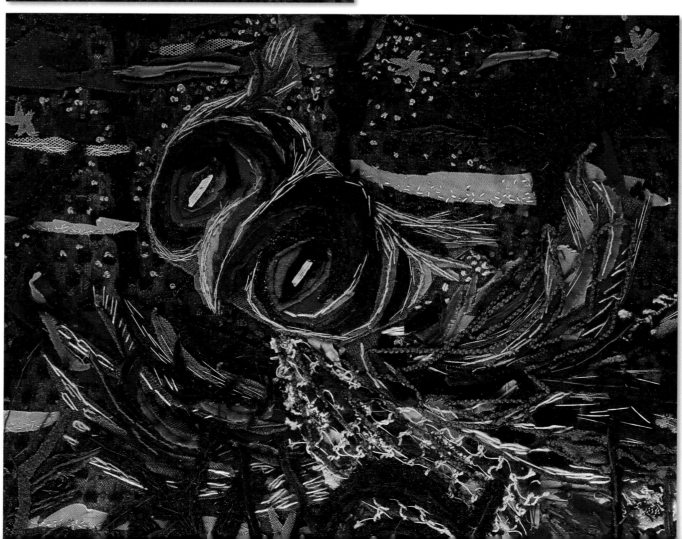

WOOD PIGEONS

TECHNIQUE: fabric appliqué, hand embroidery
DATE: 1963
PLACE of origin: England
SIZE: 70 x 31cm (27½ x 12¼in)

This piece is called 'Wood Pigeons' and shows three wood pigeons looking for food in the snow against a background of wintry trees. The wood pigeons are portrayed in applied fabrics and net on a white, slubbed, evenweave linen with hand embroidery, sequins and beads. The appliqué here is more controlled than in the piece on the previous page and, I feel, lacks the sense of movement achieved by the free appliqué of 'The Owl on a Branch'. It is the embroidery that stands out in this piece.

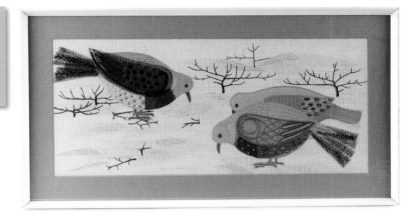

This is an examination piece. It was designed and worked for the City & Guilds examination in hand embroidery (231) in May 1963. It was gifted to the Embroiderers' Guild by the artist, who also gifted some of her design work from the same examination.

Maker: Valerie Tullock
Embroiderers' Guild number: EG1999.52

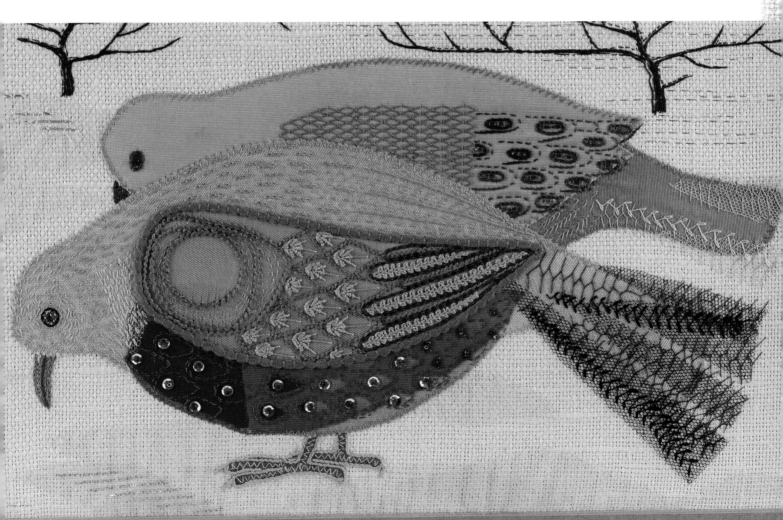

CONVERSATION PIECE

TECHNIQUE: three-dimensional machine embroidery
DATE: 1983
PLACE of origin: Great Britain
SIZE: 23 x 23cm (9 x 9in)

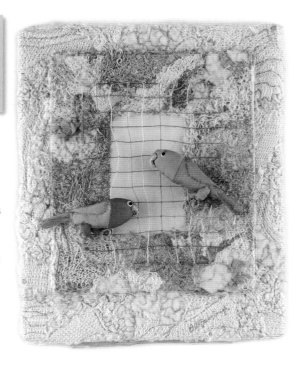

Two rather cheeky little parakeets, which are small parrots, are holding a conversation. They are made of silk, stuffed with wadding/batting and have sequins attached by beads for their eyes. They are perched on a mesh of knotted (coral stitched) silk threads, which is mounted by threading the knotted threads through holes drilled in clear Perspex.

The surrounding fabric is silk and threads, which have been machined over using free machine embroidery. The artist has signed her name in machine embroidery at the bottom of the piece. This piece was purchased from the artist in 1983.

Maker: Belinda Fairclough
Embroiderers' Guild number: EG1999.52

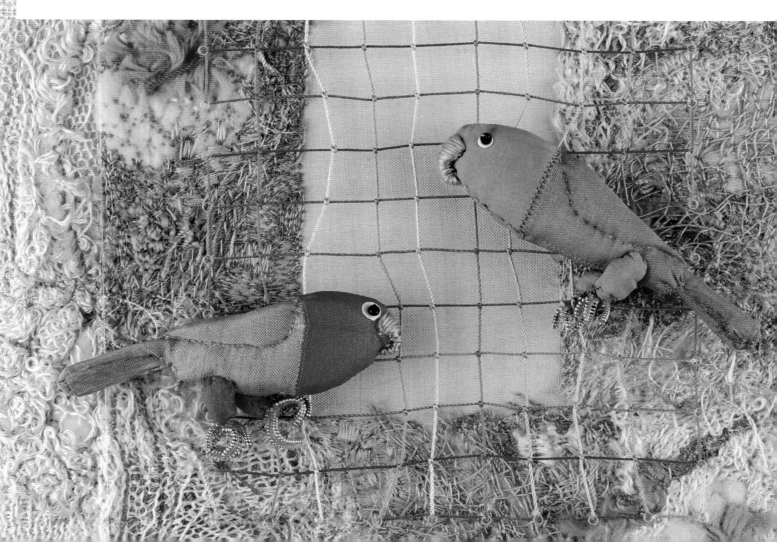

PINK PIGEON

TECHNIQUE: hand embroidery with appliqué
DATE: 1965
PLACE of origin: Great Britain
SIZE: 36 x 30cm (14¼ x 12in)

This is an early piece from the highly respected textile artist, tutor and author, Jan Beaney. Blue hessian (burlap) is the chosen background with very freely worked hand embroidery and small areas of applied fabrics. It was one of the first pieces where stitches were overlapped for textural effect and caused consternation among traditional embroiderers, who felt that Cretan stitch should only be worked in one way. Jan went on to play with stitches, resulting in one of her very popular books, *Embroidery – New Approaches*. Stitches include Cretan stitch, French knots, straight stitches and detached chain stitches. Thick and thin threads add texture and life to this pigeon.

Look back to the first bird in this chapter, 'The Owl on a Branch' (page 76), to see another freely worked interpretation of a bird.

'Pink Pigeon' was selected for a very early 1962 Group exhibition at the Embroiderers' Guild headquarters in Wimpole Street, London, and featured on the front cover of *Embroidery*, the journal of the Embroiderers' Guild – a special edition for our Diamond Jubilee in 1966.

Maker: Jan Beaney
Embroiderers' Guild number: EG1989.2

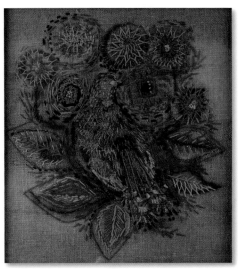

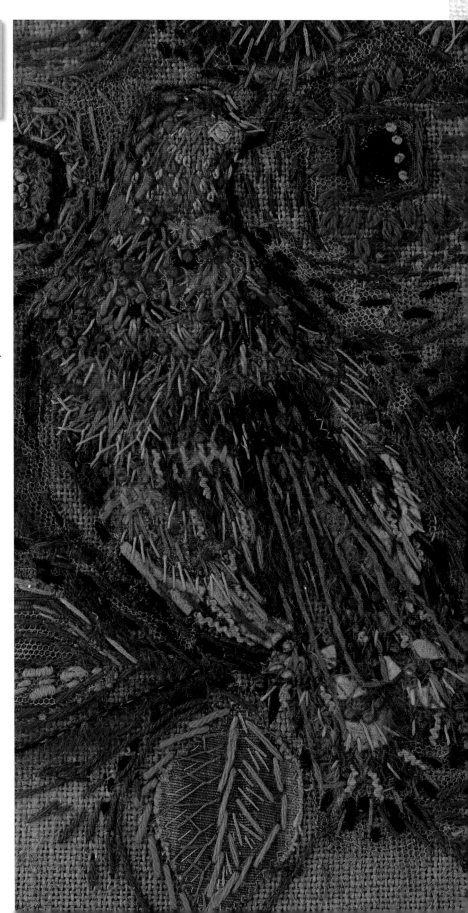

THE UNFORTUNATE BIRD

TECHNIQUE: appliqué with hand embroidery
DATE: 2014
PLACE of origin: Great Britain
SIZE: 36 x 41cm (14¼ x 16¼in)

This little bird embroidery has a sad story, as inspiration came from a bird that the artist's cat brought in. In fact, the bird looks quite cosy with its beak tucked in to its chest.

Framed in an oval mount of black velvet, the bird is stitched onto a background of synthetic lace fabric. The bird's chest is dyed and distressed muslin held down with long stitches in self-coloured thread. The head, body and wings are a heavier fabric embroidered in grey and cream cotton threads in small straight stitches. The wings are embroidered in bands of straight stitches to give the appearance of feathers. The eye and beak are worked in satin stitch with two tiny white stitches that bring the eye to life.

Jo Smith was an Embroiderers' Guild scholar in 2013. She made this piece especially for the Collection in April 2013. Her signature is on the reverse.

Maker: Jo Smith
Embroiderers' Guild number: not yet accessioned

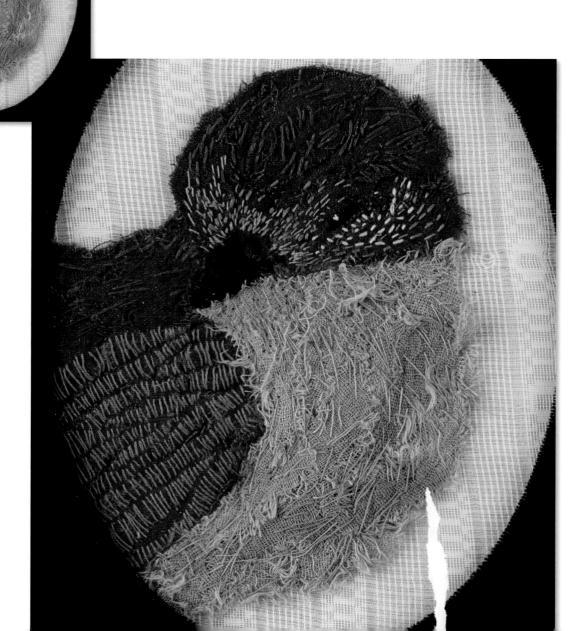

BERLIN WORK

TECHNIQUE: Berlin work, plush stitch
DATE: mid 19th century
PLACE of origin: Great Britain
SIZE: 62 x 80cm (24½ x 31½in)

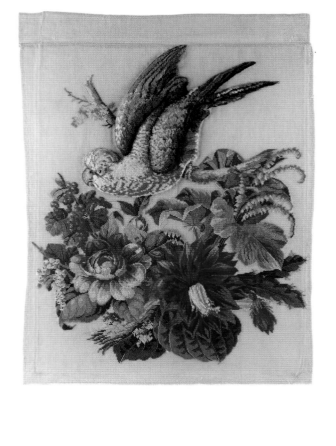

The colours in this fire screen panel are typical of the aniline dyes that became popular in the mid 19th century. These were the first synthetic dyes to be produced in factories, after a search for synthetic quinine led to the discovery of mauve, which became the first synthetic dye, followed by many others all of intense colour.

The dyes were used on the wool threads used for reproducing Berlin work charts, where squares representing stitches were coloured in the appropriate colour. The charts originated in Berlin and became overwhelmingly popular. This parrot is stitched in plush stitch, where loops of thread are secured by cross stitches and packed in to the mesh of the canvas ground fabric. Once finished, the loops are cut and the threads brushed to create a solid shape. Amateur embroiderers would sometimes send their work away to have their plush stitch professionally cut and shaped.

Although this is clearly a parrot, the tail seems rather short. Perhaps there was not enough space on the chart for a full-length tail.

Embroiderers' Guild number: EG3794

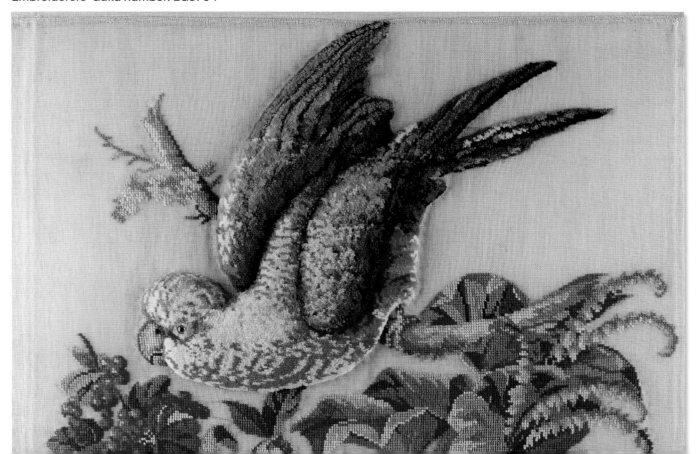

CANVAS WORK COCKEREL

TECHNIQUE: canvas work, tent stitch

DATE: mid 20th century

PLACE of origin: Great Britain

SIZE: 20 x 20cm (8 x 8in)

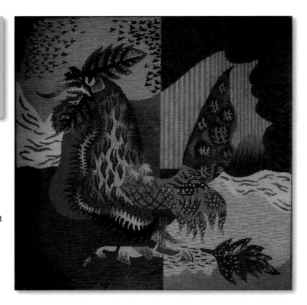

The originality of design of this cockerel panel is very clear. The bird is almost stylized, with its plumage reduced to blocks of pattern against a background of blocks of colour, which are also patterned. The background is fine canvas and the work is embroidered entirely in tent stitch using stranded cotton.

This is one of four pieces in the Embroiderers' Guild Collection by Sears and, from a label attached to another of the pieces, it seems all four might be examination work. Unfortunately, the label gives little information. 'Cockerel' is worked in a very traditional way, but it is elevated to art form by the design. Notice how the comb of the cockerel, the feathers on the wing and the leaf on the ground bear similarities in their design and colour, linking them in a diagonal across the work.

Maker: Laurence Morgan Sears
Embroiderers' Guild number: EG1983.179

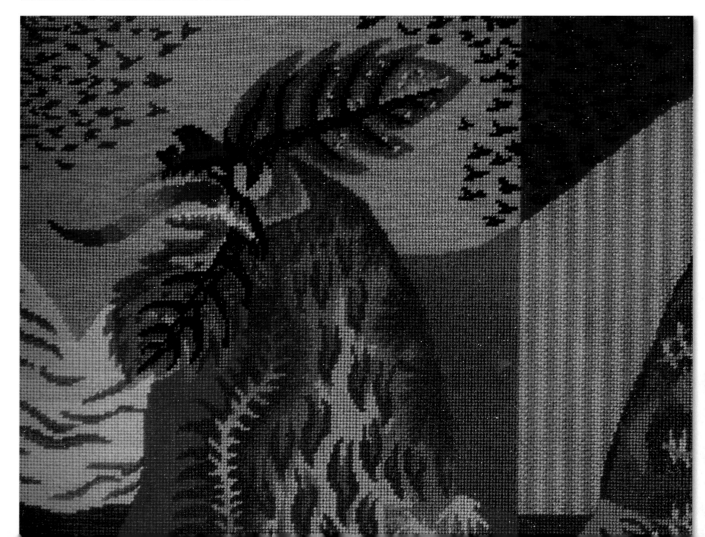

EXOTIC BIRD

TECHNIQUE: hand embroidery

DATE: mid 20th century

PLACE of origin: Great Britain or Europe

SIZE: 66 x 41cm (26 x 16¼in)

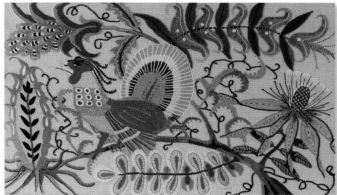

On a background of slubbed cotton is portrayed an exotic bird perched on a branch, surrounded by strange leaves and flowers. The design is stitched in stranded cotton. I can find no evidence of lines beneath the stitching, which would indicate that it is a hot iron transfer design. It is very well stitched, using chain, satin, feather, detached chain and whipped stitches. There are also bullion knots, which are made in a similar way to French knots, but where a longer needle is used and the thread is wrapped many times round the needle. The finished stitch resembles a short sausage.

I have chosen to include this as art because it is art of its time. It can be looked at and enjoyed, not just as an example of embroidery, but as a decorative object to be appreciated and admired, regardless of how it was made.

Embroiderers' Guild number: yet to be accessioned

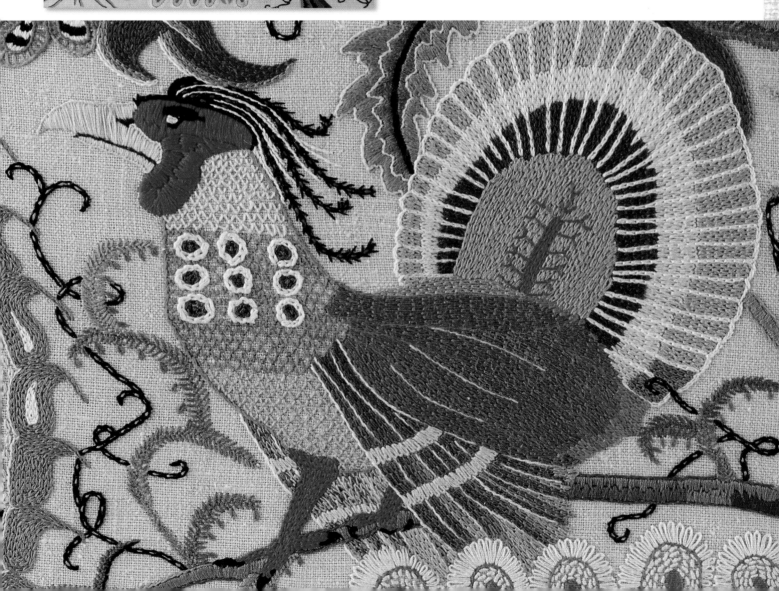

ALISON LILEY'S COCKEREL

TECHNIQUE: hand embroidery
DATE: 1962
PLACE of origin: Great Britain
SIZE: 31 x 43cm (12¼ x 17in)

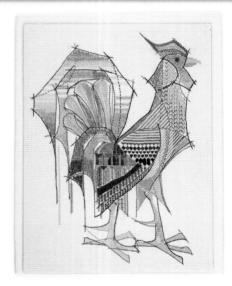

This is undoubtedly a cockerel, portrayed in a variety of hand embroidery stitches, on a white, evenweave fabric background. Stranded cotton and coton a broder have been used. The stitches are, however, used unconventionally and the technique is exemplary. So, how does this piece qualify as art?

Further research shows me that the designer and maker, Alison Liley, featured in a solo embroidery exhibition held at the Embroiderers' Guild headquarters at 51, Queen Anne Street, London in 1955, where her work was described as varied and lively. *Embroidery* magazine said it achieved 'That different look which is so much sought after', and was 'A refreshing change from the perceived traditional emphasis of the Embroiderers' Guild'. It was noted that Liley was an exponent of the contemporary school and that this was the first solo exhibition of a member's work sponsored by the Embroiderers' Guild, and that Liley more than justified the faith placed in her. So, here we have possibly the first acceptance of embroidery as art.

Maker: Alison Liley
Gifted by: Alison Liley
Embroiderers' Guild Number: EG2678

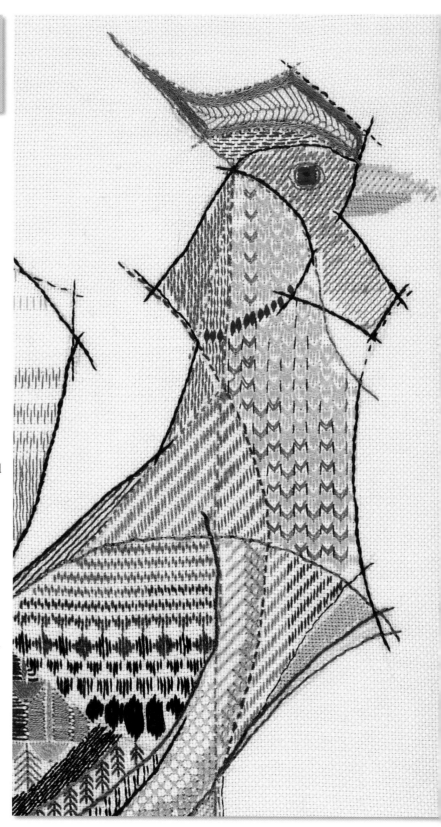

ART NOUVEAU-STYLE PANEL

TECHNIQUE: hand embroidery
DATE: 1910
PLACE of origin: Great Britain
SIZE: 51 x 35cm (20 x 13¾in)

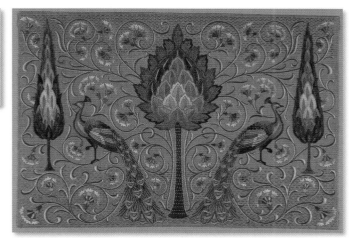

This design, Art Nouveau in style, is part of a collection of work submitted for a City & Guilds examination in 1910, for which the maker, Katherine Helena Powell, gained a silver medal.

The background is light bronze-coloured linen and the limited colour range of the embroidery, using silk thread, gives a particular unity to the work. Stitches used are buttonhole, couched threads, backstitch, stem stitch and seeding stitches. I leave it to the reader to decide whether they prefer these peacocks to the elaborate, padded, sequinned and embellished peacocks from India, seen earlier on page 23.

Powell's work is even more incredible when you consider that she was born with only one hand. During the First World War she painted numerals and letters on compasses for the Royal Flying Corps. She was a teacher of art and needlework.

Maker: Katherine Helena Powell
Gifted by: Lady Hamilton Fairley
Embroiderers' Guild Number: EG3207
Lady Hamilton Fairley was the first chairman of the Embroiderers' Guild, who organized exhibitions for them and was a teacher and lecturer in embroidery.

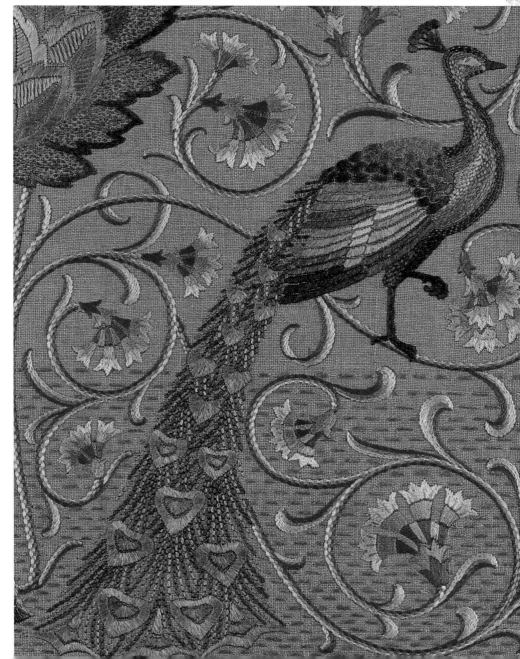

CHINESE PHEASANTS

TECHNIQUE: appliqué with hand embroidery

DATE: 1910

PLACE of origin: Great Britain

SIZE: 35 x 51cm (13¾ x 20in)

This piece is undoubtedly one of my favourite pieces in the Collection. I love the vibrant colours, the exuberant flowers and the beautifully stitched birds. The embroidery is Chinese in style, although it was made in Great Britain. Look back to page 51 and the Chinese roundel, which was stitched in China. There are similarities of style in the birds and tree in this piece. The black background brings out the vibrant colours in the design. The flowers are applied fabrics edged with satin stitch, but the pheasants are entirely hand stitched in shaded straight stitches. Notice the feathery effect on the birds' breasts and the scaly effect on the legs, achieved by straight stitches in a trellis pattern over laid threads.

Embroiderers' Guild number: not yet accessioned

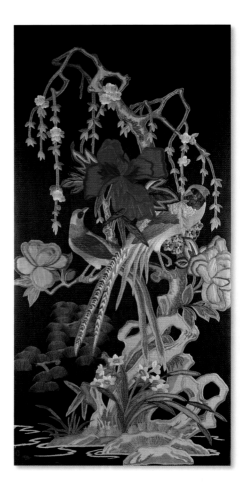

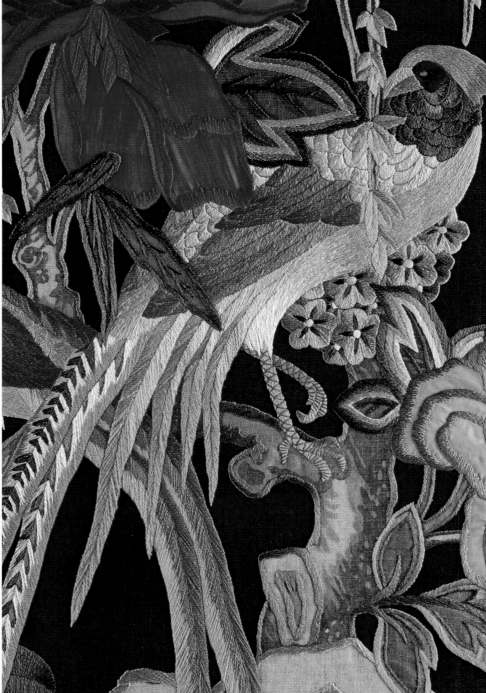

ROBIN IN A SNOW STORM

TECHNIQUE: hand and machine embroidery, collage
DATE: 1965
PLACE of origin: Great Britain
SIZE: 21cm (8¼in) in diameter

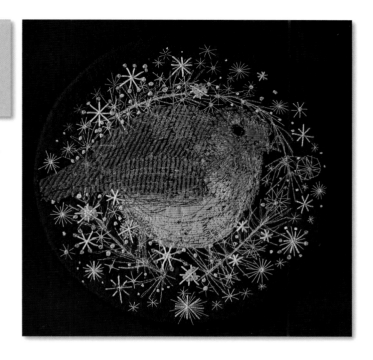

This robin has a green felt background and is a collage of textured fabrics with hand-embroidered twigs and snowflakes.

This panel was exhibited at an early exhibition of the textile art group, The 62 Group, which at this time was linked to the Embroiderers' Guild. The exhibition was held at the Guild's headquarters, which were at Wimpole Street, London. The robin was purchased from the exhibition by Miss B. Sinclair Salmon, who was then secretary of the Embroiderers' Guild. It hung in her office until she left the Guild. On her death, it was returned to the artist, Jean Carter, who promptly donated it to the Embroiderers' Guild Collection.

Maker: Jean Carter
Gifted by: Jean Carter
Embroiderers' Guild number: EG1998.13

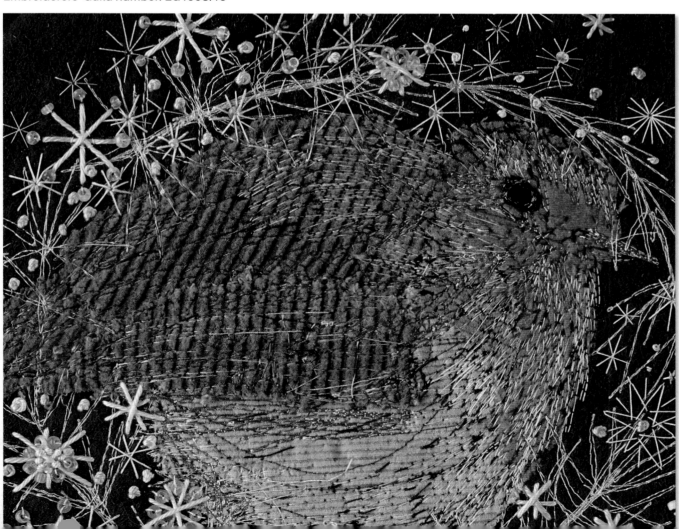

SAMPLES AND
SAMPLERS

Traditionally, a sampler is an embroidery designed to show the expertise of the embroiderer and as a reference of techniques and designs for future work.

Early samplers worked by young girls were part of their educational progress in needlework and they would progress from samplers to more ambitious projects.

From the mid 20th century, the term sampler became popular to describe pictorial embroideries in which many different stitches were used.

The Noah's Ark panels in this chapter are not samplers in the traditional sense, but are samples of embroidery demonstrating single techniques to a common theme. One sampler in this category has been made up as a bag. The other samplers in the chapter are in the traditional style from the 18th to 20th centuries.

BERLIN WORK BUDGERIGAR

TECHNIQUE: Berlin work, plush stitch
DATE: 1847
PLACE of origin: unknown
SIZE: 11.5 x 147cm (4½ x 58in)

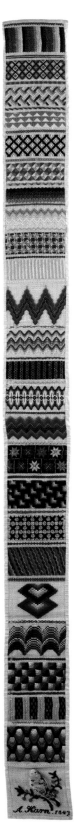

We looked at Berlin work and particularly plush stitch in the previous chapter. This is a very long, narrow sampler of patterns and stitches, made as a reference for future work. It is known as a strip sampler because the geometric designs are stitched in bands or blocks. At the bottom is a realistic budgerigar sitting amidst branches with berries. The thread used is wool.

We have no place of origin for this piece but it is known to have been donated by Essie Newberry, who gave many pieces to the Collection from many countries. To me, the name does not seem to be British and the lettering is ornate and might be European.

Maker: A. Karn
Gifted by: Essie Newberry
Embroiderers' Guild number: EG1746

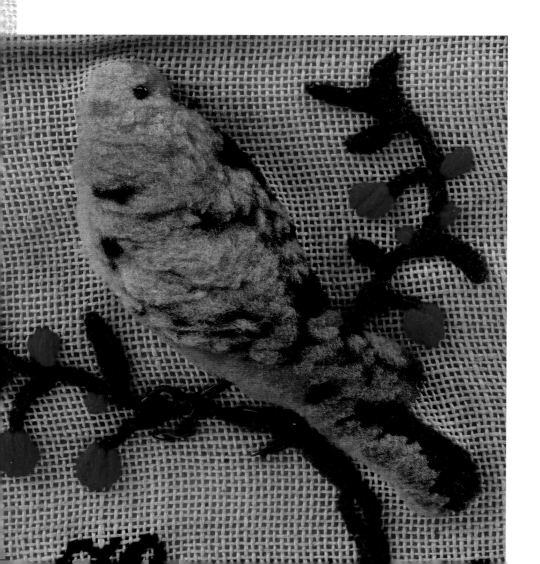

PICTORIAL SAMPLER

TECHNIQUE: counted thread

DATE: 1840

PLACE of origin: Great Britain

SIZE: 43.5 x 41cm (17 x 16¼in)

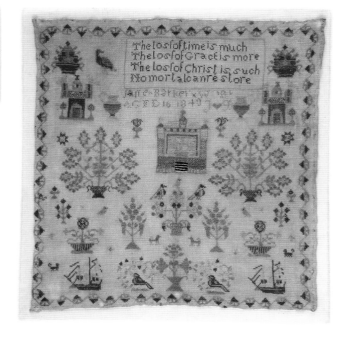

This is a pictorial sampler. Pictorial samplers can take several forms. In the 19th century and earlier, they were a series of different images within a sampler, which often told a story, but usually featured one stitch. Pictorial samplers in the 20th century were often designed as a picture where a number of stitches were used in the sampler.

This sampler is stitched on natural linen in wool and silk threads and stitched in cross stitch. Its date is very similar to A. Karn's sampler, which we have just looked at (opposite), but this sampler is not Berlin work. The colours are subdued and the sampler follows the traditions of samplers from earlier centuries. Birds in this sampler are very small and formal, perched in fruit trees. The design of this sampler is symmetrical, but look at the verse panel at the top. It is slightly off-centre. Could the bird to the left of the panel be an added extra to fill a gap left by the misplaced verse panel?

Maker: Jane Barker (aged 16)
Embroiderers' Guild number: EG5805

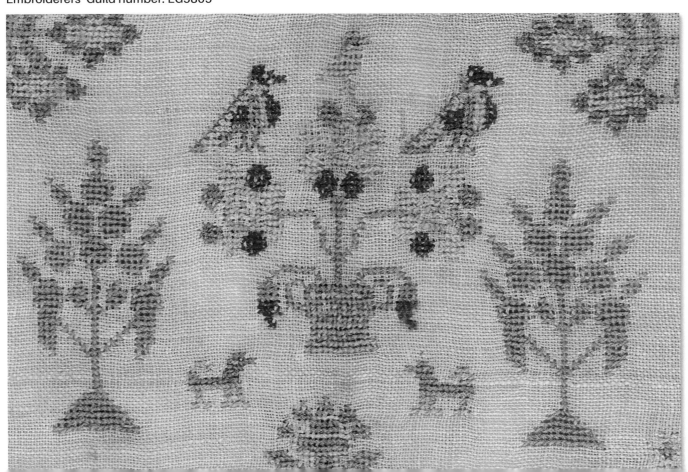

THE FALCONER SAMPLER

TECHNIQUE: counted thread
DATE: 17th century
PLACE of origin: Great Britain
SIZE: 22.5 x 55cm (8¾ x 21½in)

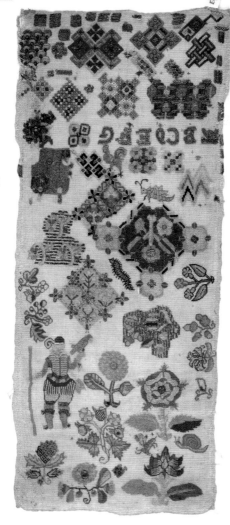

This is a very rare spot sampler, where small motifs are stitched apparently randomly on a background fabric. It is one of only two depictions of a falconer and falcon. The other is in the Goodhart Collection at Montacute House, Somerset, UK. This sampler is not dated but it is typical of 16th to 17th century samplers, especially the clothing of the falconer.

Here, we concentrate on the two birds within the sampler; the falcon itself and a cockerel, just below the lettering, who seems to be striding forwards with a determined look. The fabric of the sampler is natural linen and the thread used on the two birds is silk. The stitching is in petit point canvas work. The falcon is spotted and appears to have a beak slightly out of proportion to its body. The eye looks slightly benign compared to the fierce gaze associated with birds of prey. The cockerel is realistically portrayed with a bright red comb and coloured tail feathers.

This sampler was found during a chance visit to an antique shop by G. Ella Russell in 1950. Ella states in an article in *Embroidery* magazine that the sampler was very reasonably priced. It eventually reached the Embroiderers' Guild Collection via Mrs Wharton, who was a niece of G. Ella Russell.

Gifted by: Mrs Wharton
Embroiderers' Guild number: EG1999.17

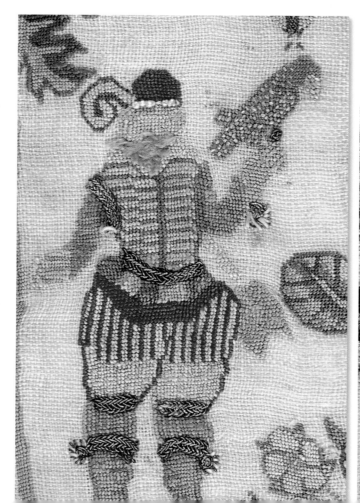

SOLANGE CARLOT SAMPLER

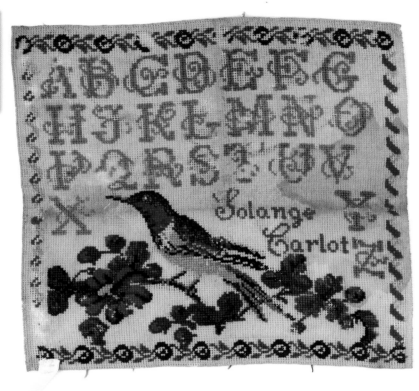

TECHNIQUE: counted thread

DATE: 19th century

PLACE of origin: France

SIZE: 24 x 20cm (9½ x 8in)

This sampler was purchased from an internet auction site in 2015. It is worked on canvas in the wool threads and colours typical of Berlin work. The stitch used is tent stitch.

The name Solange is French, so the sampler may hail from France; the lettering is very ornate as well, which might indicate a European origin. Unfortunately, there is no provenance for this piece and the seller was unable to provide further information.

With its long, pointed beak and bright plumage, the subject may be a hummingbird.

Embroiderers' Guild number: not yet accessioned

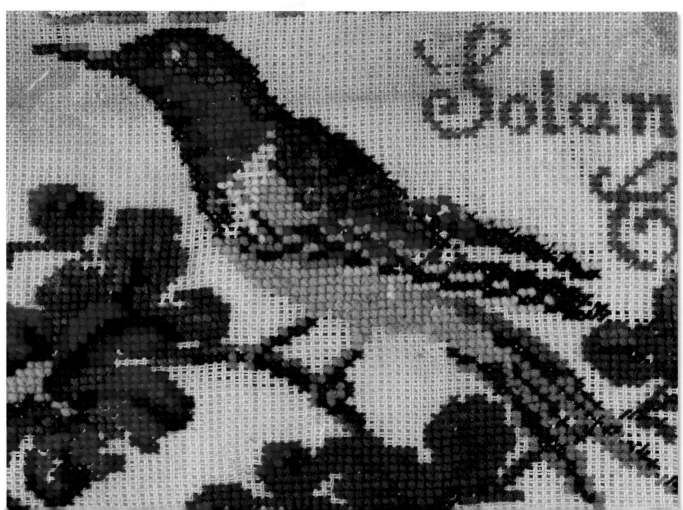

PEACOCK SAMPLER

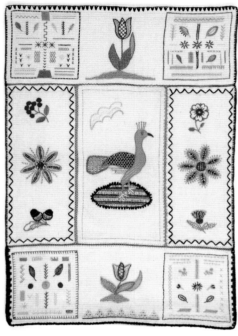

TECHNIQUE: hand embroidery

DATE: mid 20th century

PLACE of origin: Great Britain

SIZE: 26.5 x 38.5cm (10½ x 15¼in)

Here we have a British interpretation of a peacock in a pictorial sampler of many stitches. Interestingly, this sampler has been backed with fabric and made up as a bag. Darning and laid thread techniques can be seen on the peacock, which seems to be standing in a pond of straight stitches. The fabric is cotton and the threads are stranded cotton.

This sampler is one of our untraced finds, discovered in the Collection during cataloguing. We do not know who made it or how it arrived in the Collection.

Embroiderers' Guild number: EG5198

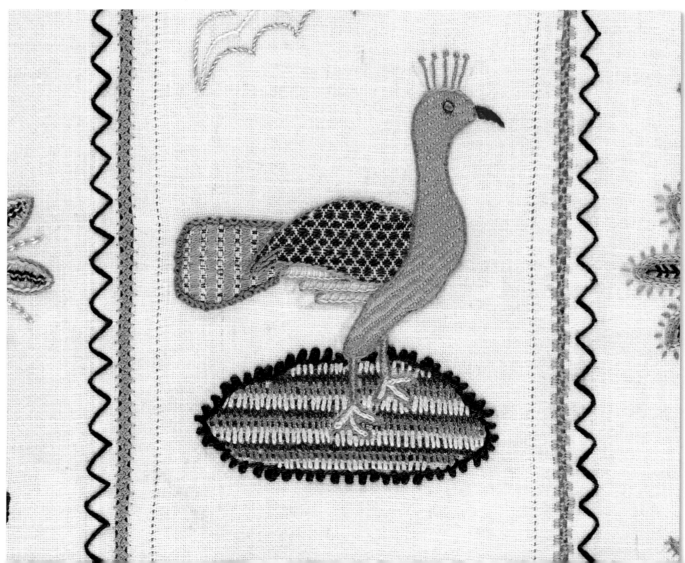

ANN RATHMELL SAMPLER

TECHNIQUE: counted thread
DATE: 1788
PLACE of origin: Great Britain
SIZE: 32 x 37cm (12½ x 14½in)

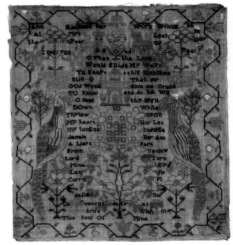

The first thing that strikes the reader about this sampler is its poor condition. The colours have faded extensively and the linen background is discoloured and holed.

Fortunately, Ann Rathmell has chosen to portray two unusually large birds, one either side of a verse, which is itself unusual as it is divided in two between the top and bottom lines by a building and floral motifs. The threads are silk and the stitches are tent stitch and satin stitch. It is quite difficult to work out what these birds might be, but they do have very long peacock-like tails.

At the top of the sampler is stitched 'Ann Rathmell her work wrought at Mrs Leas in the year of our Lord 1788'. Her age is too indistinct to read. I wonder if Mrs Leas was her school teacher, or perhaps an embroidery tutor?

Maker: Ann Rathmell
Embroiderers' Guild number: EG4165

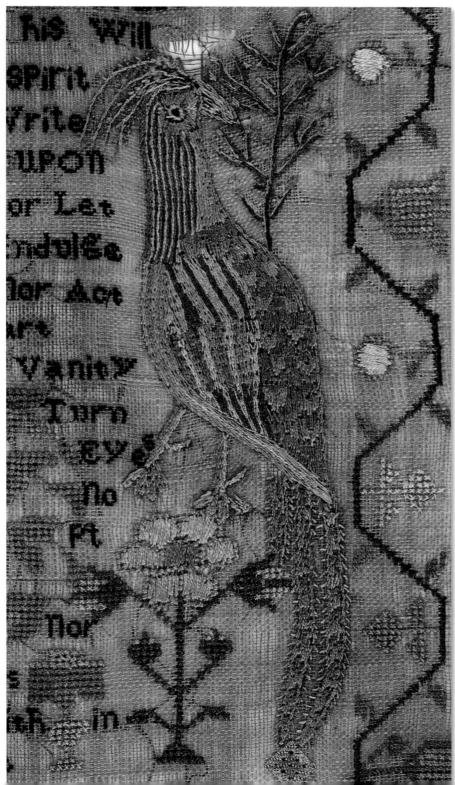

BERLIN WORK SAMPLER

TECHNIQUE: counted thread
DATE: mid 19th century
PLACE of origin: Great Britain
SIZE: 116 x 17cm (45½ x 6¾in)

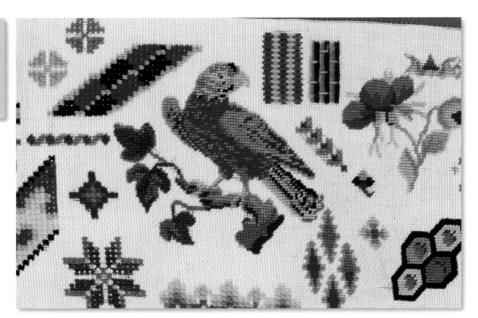

This very long sampler can be compared to the one we saw earlier on page 90. They are both examples of Berlin work, but A. Karn's sampler is a band sampler, whereas this is a spot sampler where motifs are placed at random, rather than as bands of stitches.

Here, there is no name stitched on the sampler. It is a good example of a spot sampler with numerous small images crammed into the available space, displaying a variety of stitches. It is a lovely example of Berlin work on canvas with the characteristic bright wool thread and two birds, including a parrot, perched on a branch, looking somewhat surprised. Both are dwarfed by a huge butterfly.

Embroiderers' Guild number: EG586

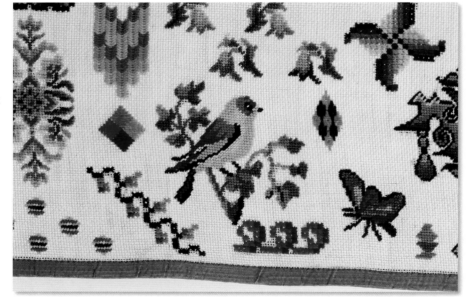

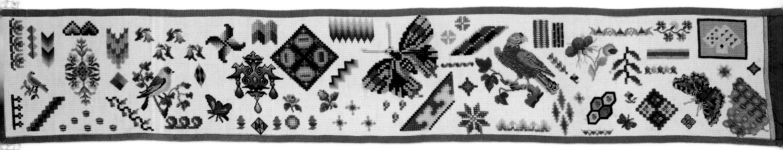

NOAH'S ARK PANELS

TECHNIQUE: hand embroidery
DATE: 1950s
PLACE of origin: Great Britain
SIZE: 20 x 32cm (8 x 12½in)

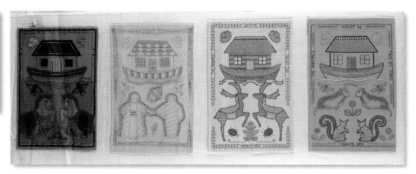

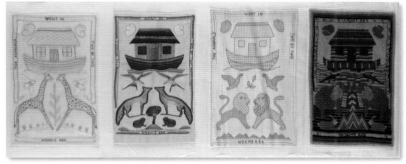

These birds are from two panels in a series of eight representing Noah's Ark and the animals going in two by two. Each panel is a sampler of a different technique on natural linen. All eight panels are shown here, but the two details are from the bottom row, panels 6 and 7. The detail below left is from panel 6, featuring two colourful birds in straight stitches. This panel demonstrates coloured embroidery. The detail below right is from panel 7, featuring two birds in pulled fabric embroidery, and demonstrates pulled fabric embroidery.

These panels were made by members of the North East branch of the Embroiderers' Guild in response to a competition to make eight samples of embroidery in any design to a foolscap size (originally 8½ x 13½in/21.5 x 34.25cm). Foolscap was eventually replaced by what we now know as A4. The branch won first prize for their Noah's Ark panels.

Panel 6:
Maker: N. Mole
Embroiderers' Guild number (below left): EG1982.9.7

Panel 7:
Maker: L. A. Davies
Embroiderers' Guild number (below right): EG1982.9.6

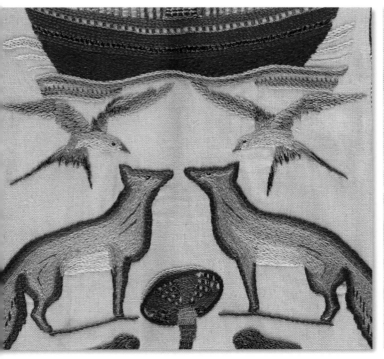

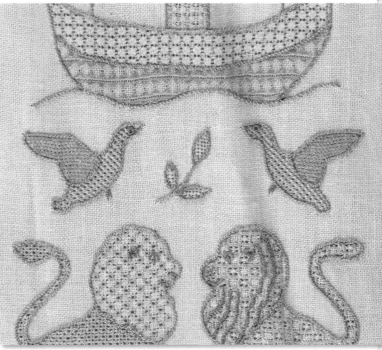

FANCIFUL BIRDS

T he birds in this chapter stand out for being different and not recognizable as particular species. Some are mythical, some imaginative and there are other examples elsewhere in this book, especially in Chinese embroidery. I particularly like the cushion cover representing staff at Embroiderers' Guild headquarters and Alison Liley's 'Birdcage', which could not possibly accommodate those large birds.

CANVAS WORK CUSHION COVER

TECHNIQUE: counted thread
DATE: 1960
PLACE of origin: Great Britain
SIZE: 45 x 45cm (17¾ x 17¾in)

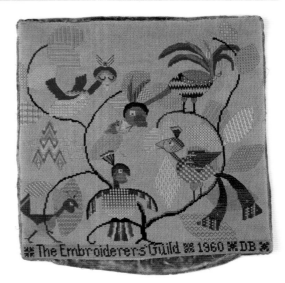

This is one of my favourite pieces, simply because of the story behind it. These are not just any birds; they represent the Embroiderers' Guild staff in 1960. At that time, our address was 56, Queen Anne Street, London W1. The accommodation was considered to be quite inadequate and a successful expansion fund had been launched to find more suitable premises in central London. Our secretary was Miss B. Sinclair Salmon, and I feel sure she is one of the birds on this cushion cover.

The design is stitched using Appleton's crewel wool in a variety of canvas work stitches. The background is brick stitch. Unfortunately, I have been unable to identify the members of staff represented by these birds. Miss Sinclair Salmon, as secretary of the Embroiderers' Guild in the 1960s, is a name that crops up quite often in the memories of Guild members. Her initial is given as B. but I don't know what the B stands for. Similarly, there is no record of the Christian name of Mrs D. Brittain. It was very uncommon for Christian names to be used in the early life of the Embroiderers' Guild and this was still the case in the 1960s when staff members, makers and tutors were always addressed formally. By the late 1980s when I was doing City & Guilds courses in embroidery, this was no longer the case and everyone was on Christian name terms.

Maker: Mrs D. Brittain
Embroiderers' Guild number: EG5318

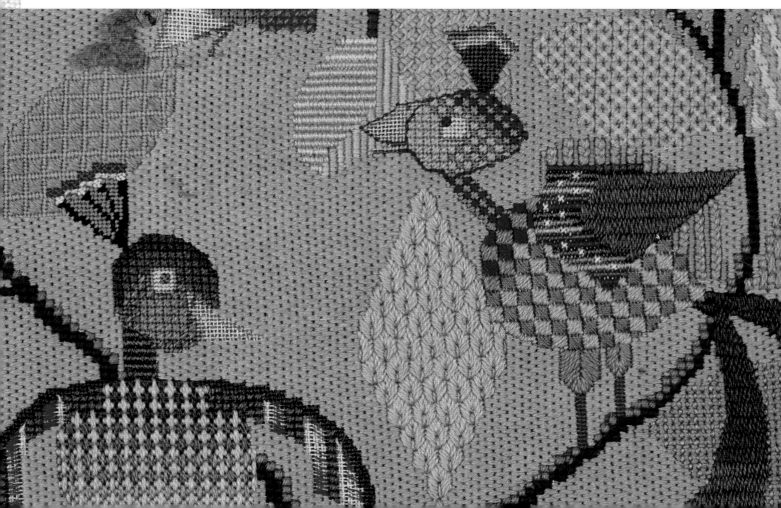

PATTERN DARNING

TECHNIQUE: pattern darning
DATE: 1958
PLACE of origin: Great Britain
SIZE: 31 x 38.5cm (12¼ x 15¼in)

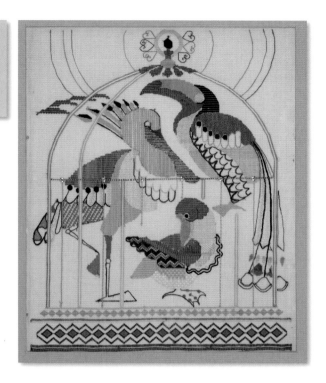

Look back to page 84 in chapter 8, where you will find Alison Liley's 'Cockerel'. 'Birdcage' is another artwork by the same artist and is certainly fanciful, as three birds squashed in to a cage like this would not be sitting quietly.

The fabric is stiffened silk gauze with silk threads and pattern darning. Pattern darning is made by inserting a needle and thread in and out of the threads of the background fabric, creating lines of varying lengths, which form a pattern of stitches. It is a much more delicate version of the sock darning technique, rarely used nowadays. The birds have applied paste jewels for eyes.

Maker: Alison Liley
Gifted by: Alison Liley
Embroiderers' Guild number: EG3010

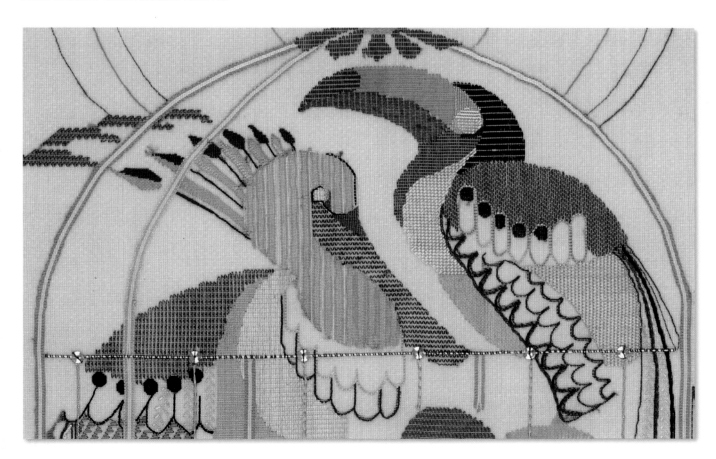

MYTHICAL BIRD

TECHNIQUE: hand embroidery

DATE: 1971

PLACE of origin: Great Britain

SIZE: 40.5 x 52cm (16 x 20½in)

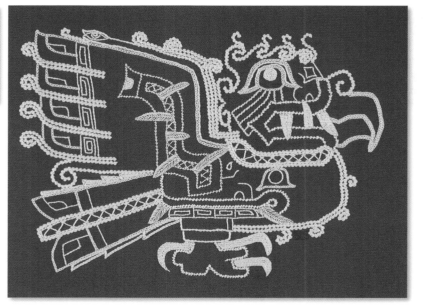

We looked at Barbara Snook's 'Cockerel' in the first chapter of this book. The colours used in this mythical bird are also white threads on a red background, but there is a greater variety of stitches. They include feather stitch, stem stitch chain stitch, whipped running stitch and coral stitch. Look closely under the body of the bird, to the right of the claws, and you may just be able to see that Barbara has embroidered her initials in the same red as the background fabric: BLS.

Maker: Barbara Snook
Gifted by: Jean Carter
Embroiderers' Guild number: EG2014.2

SEA EAGLE

TECHNIQUE: hand embroidery

DATE: 1971

PLACE of origin: Great Britain

SIZE: 55 x 42cm (21½ x 16½in)

This is a third example of Barbara Snook's work and another strange bird, which she named 'Sea Eagle'. This one is very colourful – more so than the pieces we looked at earlier – but the use of a bright background and beautiful hand stitchery is the same. Barbara has used thick and thin threads to add texture to this piece. Some white thread is very fine and has been used for the shapes outside the bird's body. The background fabric is a textured furnishing fabric. Barbara's initials can be seen beneath the claw in fine black thread. Stranded cotton has been used for the embroidery, which includes chain stitch, fly stitch, Cretan stitch and satin stitch.

This piece was stitched specially for an illustration in one of Barbara's books, *Embroidery Designs from Pre-Columbian Art* (Charles Scribner's Sons, 1975).

Maker: Barbara Snook
Gifted by: Jean Carter
Embroiderers' Guild number: EG2014.43

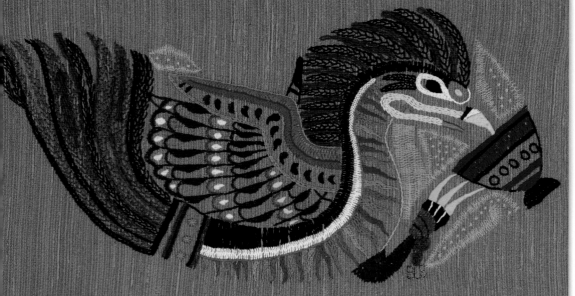

EXUBERANT BIRDS

TECHNIQUE: crewel embroidery style
DATE: 20th century
PLACE of origin: Great Britain
SIZE: 28 x 20cm (11 x 8in)

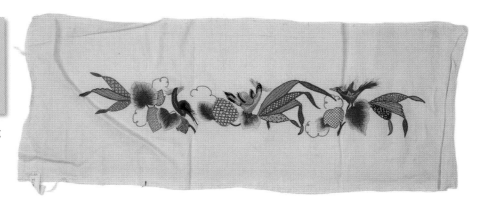

These three birds, joyfully singing among leaves with clouds in the sky (or possibly tendrils), do not resemble any species that I have come across and I feel they have come from the imagination of the embroiderer. The background fabric is linen and the birds are embroidered in silk in straight, shaded stitches. The red bird on the right looks particularly feathery.

The filling stitches on the leaves are the reason I have described this fragment as crewel embroidery style. The design looks British and I think it is 20th century. However, this is another example of an untraced find in the Embroiderers' Guild Collection.

Embroiderers' Guild number: not yet accessioned

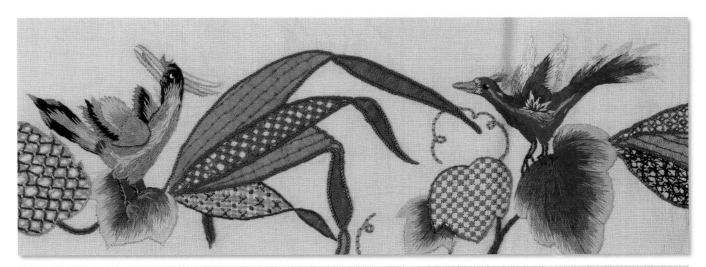

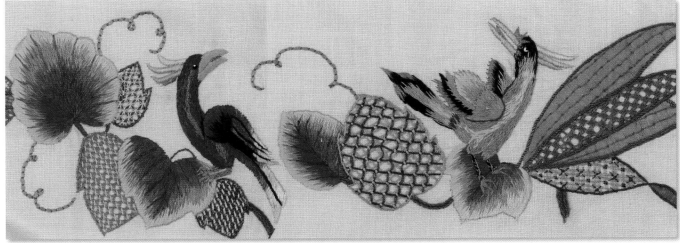

BIRDS FROM
MANY LANDS

This chapter includes gorgeous birds from India, Italy, Greece, Crete, Egypt, Hungary and China. It features the oldest pieces in the Embroiderers' Guild Collection. These are not embroideries but Coptic weavings from the 6th Century, found in shallow graves where they were preserved in the hot, dry conditions of Egypt.

Chinai work was made by Chinese immigrants who settled in India. Embroideries from Greece and the Greek Islands form a large part of the Collection with their distinctive floral and bird designs.

Most of the embroidery from this area has come to us via Guild members who specialized in Greek embroidery and built up personal collections as they researched their subject.

CHINAI WORK

TECHNIQUE: Chinai work

DATE: 19th century

PLACE of origin: India

SIZE: (cockerels) 33 x 5cm (13 x 2in);
(coloured birds) 38 x 5cm (15 x 2in)

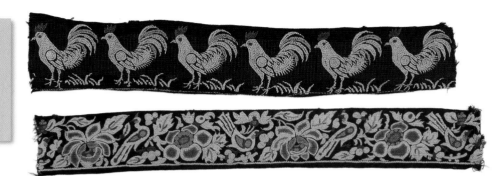

Chinai (which means Chinese) work was done by Chinese immigrants to India from the 19th century and into the 20th century. There was a community of Chinese embroiderers who lived in Surat, South Gujarat.

Their embroideries had Chinese characteristics of design and technique and were often narrow bands or borders of fine floss silk embroidery in a variety of stitches, often with bird designs. The bands were particularly suited to the Indian market, as they could be sewn on to saris or other clothing and were particularly popular among the wealthy Parsee community.

These two examples show straight stitches and knot stitches, which are traditional stitches found in Chinese embroidery. The cockerels are stitched in straight stitches and fine Pekin knots. The birds on the purple strip are stitched entirely in knot stitches, but these are less fine than Pekin knots and are characterized by little loops formed with the knot.

Embroiderers' Guild numbers: (cockerels) EG2297.1;
(coloured birds) EG4379

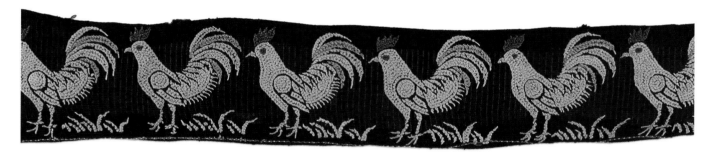

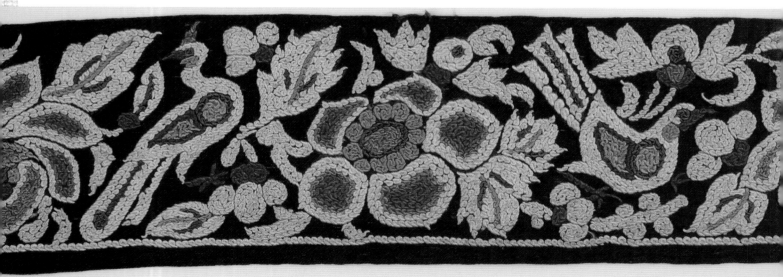

CHINAI TUNIC

TECHNIQUE: Chinai work
DATE: 19th century
PLACE of origin: India
SIZE: 50 x 51cm (19¾ x 20in)

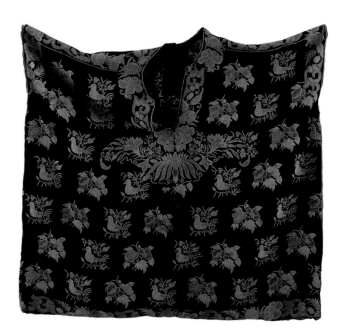

This piece is a tunic fragment and is mounted on a linen panel, which includes three short strips of Chinai work, including the cockerel strip seen on the previous page.

Not all Chinai work was embroidered in strips and this is an example. Bird motifs are embroidered on a dark blue satin background. I particularly like these birds because each motif is slightly different. Look at the birds' beaks; they are all slightly different and one appears to have a curly beak, as though it has collided with something. It is a sure sign that something is hand embroidered and not made by machine, when differences can be seen within motifs, which at first glance appear similar. The stitches are Pekin knots.

Embroiderers' Guild number: EG4862

WOOLLEN APRON

TECHNIQUE: wool embroidery
DATE: 1870
PLACE of origin: Italy
SIZE: 92 x 58cm (36¼ x 22¾in)

In the first catalogue published by the Embroiderers' Guild Permanent Collection in 1971, when there were 416 pieces, this is described as a peasant apron. However, in our most recent computer catalogue, it is described as a cloth or mat. It is a rectangular cloth with embroidery in borders at either end. The background is a dark green, woollen fabric and the threads used are also wool. The stitches are straight stitches.

I call this piece 'the black cockerels' because they are very distinctive among a riot of predominantly red flowers. The design is symmetrical and the two cockerels either side of a stylized flower make for an interesting design idea. The border is in the form of a wide band, which has been applied to the apron. The cockerels are densely stitched with straight stitches with the tail outlined in red threads, couched with yellow threads. The birds do have wings, which seem almost to be detached from the birds' bodies, but are stitched in light and dark grey threads, making them look quite feathery. In their beaks, the birds hold large flowering twigs.

Gifted by: Laura Pesel, daughter of Louisa Pesel, the first president of the Embroiderers' Guild
Embroiderers' Guild number: EG2151

17TH CENTURY PANEL FROM CRETE

TECHNIQUE: hand embroidery

DATE: 17th century

PLACE of origin: Crete (Greece)

SIZE: 38 x 36cm (15 x 14¼in)

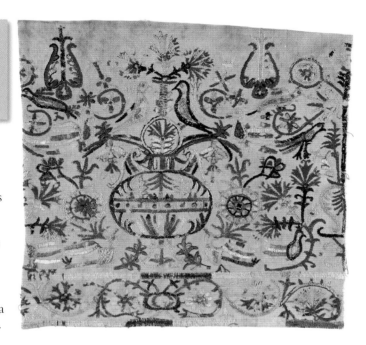

There is a lot of thread loss on this untraced find, but it is over 300 years old. It comes from Crete, the largest of the Greek islands. We have a number of very old pieces from Crete in the Collection and this one is typical of the designs that we find. This bird looks startled. Notice how it is not finely worked and there is little detail, just a blue outline with a red and yellow wing, eye and collar. There is one leg, in straight stitches and red thread.

The background is natural linen and the threads are silk with embroidery in straight or satin stitches. It is an example of embroidery that was made domestically for a purpose, but our catalogue describes it as simply a cloth.

Embroiderers' Guild number: EG312

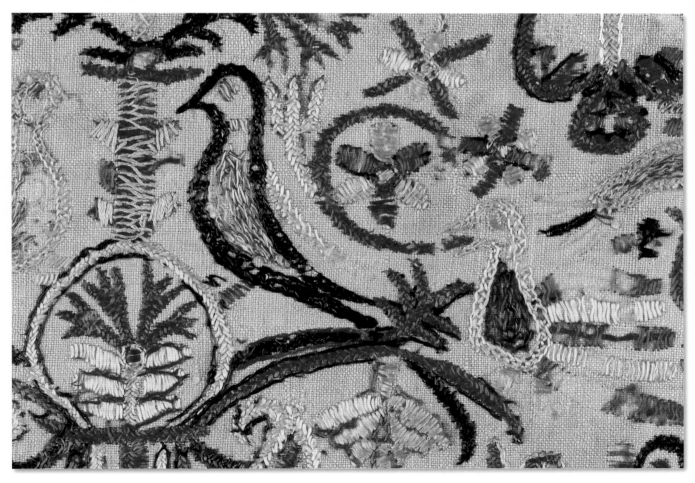

COPTIC WEAVING

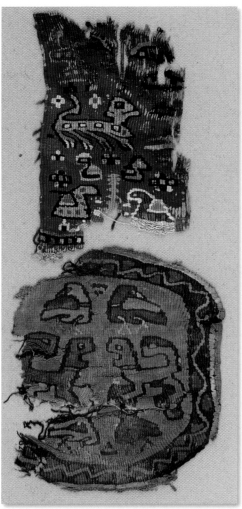

TECHNIQUE: weaving

DATE: 6th century

PLACE of origin: Egypt

SIZE: top fragment: 8.5 x 14cm (3½ x 5½in); bottom fragment: 12 x 14cm (4¾ x 5½in)

These two small fragments are without doubt the oldest pieces in the Embroiderers' Guild Collection. They are not embroidered, but woven. The two pieces are mounted together on the same board and are examples of Coptic tapestry weaving. The weavings are in linen and wool threads. The birds are described as ducks. This is quite clear on the lower fragment but less so on the upper fragment, although the shapes do have wings and feet.

The Copts were Egyptian Christians and it is due to their custom of burying the dead in their personal clothing that a surprising number of these pieces have survived. They were buried in shallow, sandy graves, sometimes in a small, brick vault and this, combined with the desert climate, helped to preserve the textiles.

Sadly, there is no provenance for these pieces. We do not know who donated them or when.

Embroiderers' Guild numbers: (top fragment) EG3856; (bottom fragment) EG3857

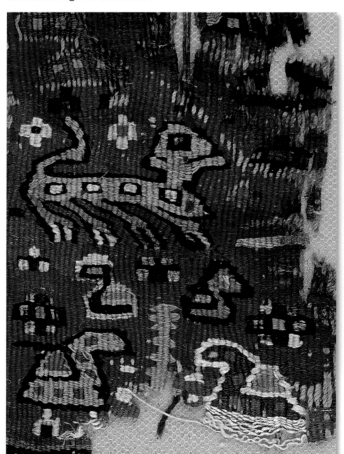

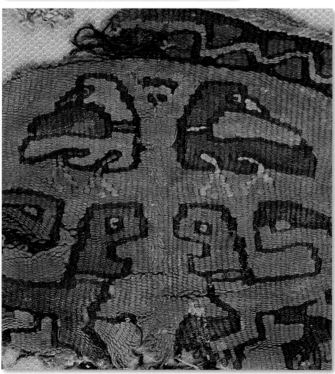

LEATHER TOBACCO POUCH

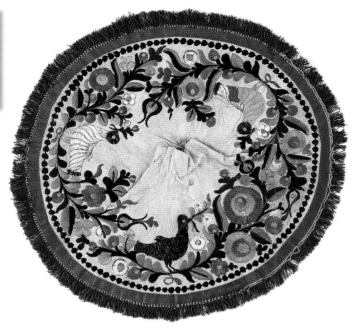

TECHNIQUE: embroidery on leather
DATE: 19th century
PLACE of origin: Hungary
SIZE: 40cm (15¾in) in diameter

I do like embroidery on leather and this is a very appealing design of birds and flowers on natural leather in silk threads. The stitches are straight stitches and in some areas threads have been lost and you can see the original needle holes. Where black threads have been used, the background leather can be seen between the stitches.

Notice how the birds all have leafy twigs in their beaks. Information about this piece comes from an index card. When the Embroiderers' Guild Collection was started, all records were handwritten onto cards, which have long disappeared, but some of the information was transferred to computer descriptions. In this example, the index card described this piece as part of a tobacco pouch; this being a decorative top, which would hang outside a waistcoat pocket. I am not sure how this would work. Further information from the index card states that the pouch comes from the Great Plain area of Hungary, between the rivers Danube and Tisza. Pieces such as this were made by local leather workers, who also made sheepskin cloaks.

Embroiderers' Guild number: EG4761

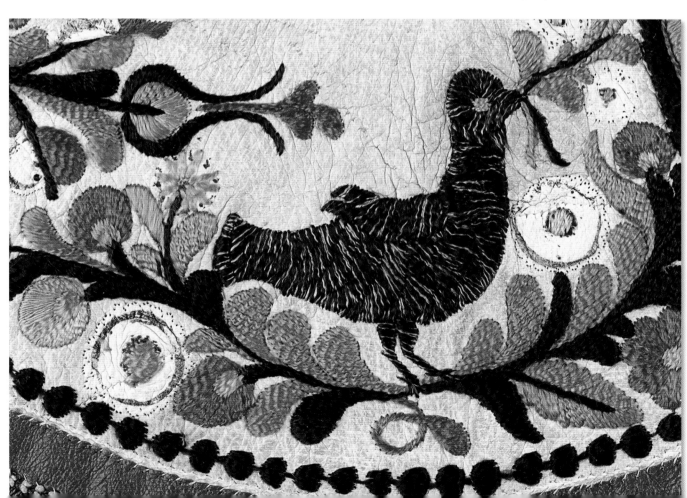

19TH CENTURY KANTHA

TECHNIQUE: kantha quilting
DATE: 1875
PLACE of origin: East Bengal (Jessore)
SIZE: 112 x 85cm (44 x 33½in)

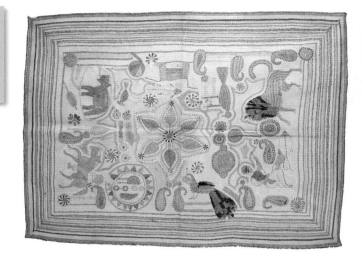

This piece is from Asia and features the fascinating tradition of kantha quilting. The technique originated in Jessore, East Bengal, which is modern-day Bangladesh. These covers were made from waste fabrics – an example of early recycling.

The technique was developed during the 19th century among low-caste Hindu washerwomen who recycled cotton saris that had become too fragile to withstand the vigorous washing process. Several saris were layered together and, using cotton threads withdrawn from the original saris, whirling patterns were made using tiny running stitches to quilt the layers together.

Designs were plants, animals and traditional Hindu symbols. Because old saris were used, the colour range in the kantha quilts was often limited to blue and red. In this piece, where the design to note is once again of a peacock, we can see orange and black threads. Notice how the wings and tail of the peacock were embroidered after the quilting had been finished, using satin stitch in blocks to represent feathers. Compare this to the second peacock, which is more stylized and stitched entirely in running stitch.

This kantha quilt was purchased from an oriental textiles dealer in London in 1983.

Embroiderers' Guild number: EG1983.5

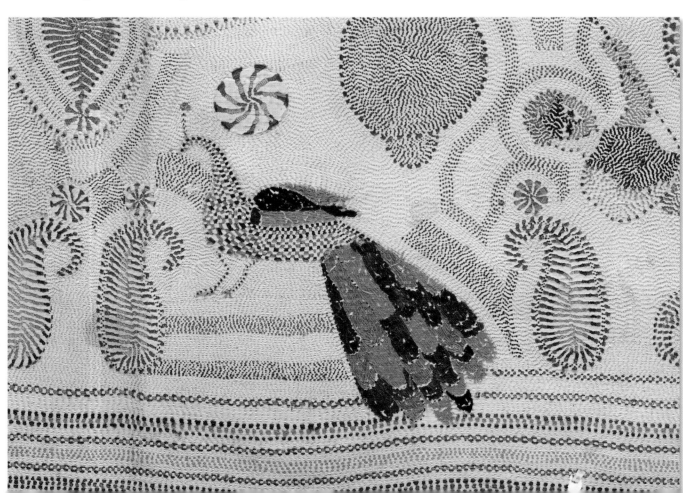

21ST CENTURY KANTHA

TECHNIQUE: kantha quilting
DATE: early 21st century
PLACE of origin: India
SIZE: 46 x 43cm (18 x 17in)

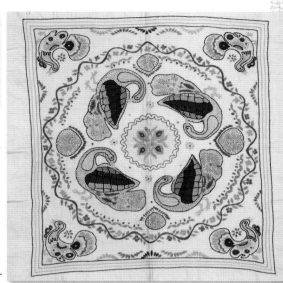

The popularity of kanthas among collectors has led to their present-day commercial production for the tourist market and they are now found in many markets and shops in India and Bangladesh.

Notice the differences between this kantha and the older one on the opposite page. The first impression is of bright colours on a clean, white background and, although the quilting technique of running stitches is the same and the peacock's wings are stitched in the same way, there is much more surface embroidery in the design. The design is much more formal compared to old kanthas, and the peacocks on the new kantha all look the same, whereas the motifs appear almost random on the fabric in older designs.

Embroiderers' Guild number: EG2014.93

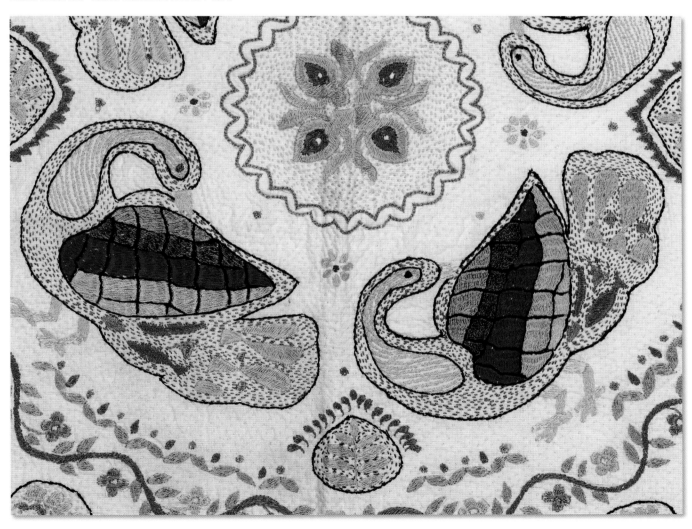

DOUBLE-HEADED EAGLE

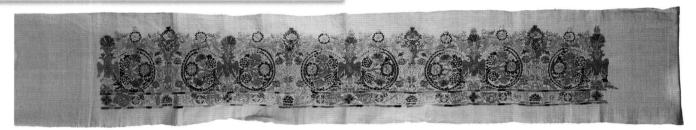

TECHNIQUE: hand embroidery

DATE: 19th century

PLACE of origin: Crete (Greece)

SIZE: 123 x 40cm (48½ x 15¾in)

Greek Island embroidery is influenced by Byzantium (Turkey), Persia (Iran) and the Middle East. Crete was ruled by the Venetians for longer than the other Greek islands and this introduced more variety of patterns and designs. A comparison can be made between the designs on Cretan skirt borders and lace borders from Venice. Traditional skirts were very full and gathered and many existing embroideries are skirt borders. Birds were a favourite design, executed in Cretan, split, satin, chain and herringbone stitches in floss silk on linen fabric. Cretan stitch is rather like

feather stitch and can be used as a dense filling stitch, or more openly.

The double-headed eagle seen on this skirt border is looking to the East and West. It was the imperial symbol of Byzantium. During the Turkish occupation, the people came to associate it with the freedom of their country. The eagle is stylized and, interestingly, although eagles are found in the mountains, naturalistic eagles with just one head do not appear in Greek embroidery.

Embroiderers' Guild number: EG2724

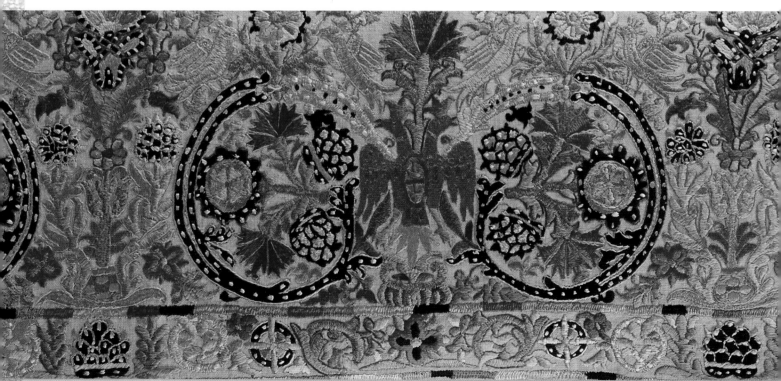

HERON WALL HANGING

TECHNIQUE: silk and metal thread embroidery

DATE: late 19th century

PLACE of origin: Japan

SIZE: 146 x 138cm (57½ x 54¼in)

The second of our Meiji period hangings is just as distinctive as the first. The background fabric is gold satin, on which are portrayed herons in a stream, among rushes and reeds. The threads are floss silk and the stitches are long and short stitch, which produces a beautiful shaded effect. Look how it enhances the birds' feathers. The herons are depicted in a very realistic way, with their bright, alert eyes, preparing for flight or fishing in the water. Neither hanging is very colourful, allowing the silk and gold threads to produce a sumptuous effect as the light plays upon them. Compare this hanging to the peacock panel on page 49, which is also Meiji work from Japan.

Embroiderers' Guild number: EG2105

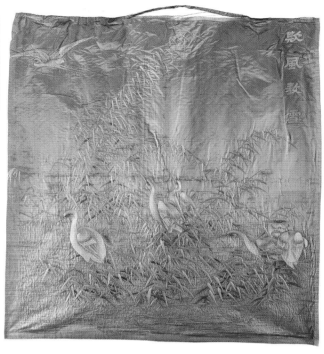

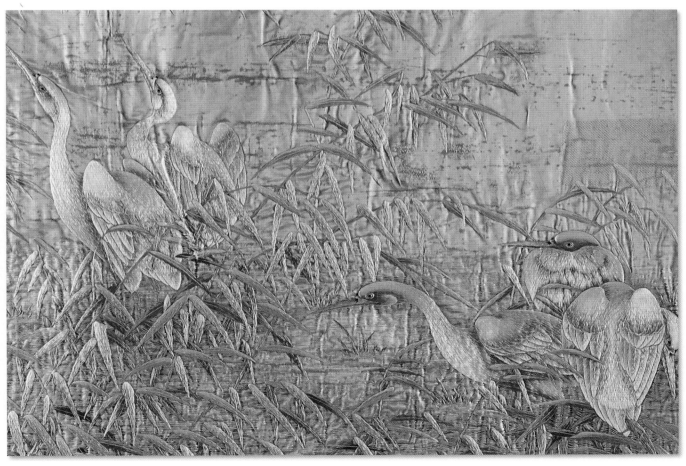

SKIRT BORDER FRAGMENT

TECHNIQUE: hand embroidery

DATE: 19th century

PLACE of origin: Crete (Greece)

SIZE: 28 x 11cm (11 x 4¼in)

This is a final example of embroidery from Crete. It is just a fragment mounted on a card this time, but almost certainly from a skirt border.

The birds here are distinctly peacocks, but the more interesting feature of this design is the characteristic mermaid with a double tail, half held in each hand, which is flanked by the two stylized peacocks. Look how lacking in character these peacocks are. They are depicted in very muted colours for peacocks. However, they do have long tails and crests on top of their heads.

Embroiderers' Guild number: EG2418

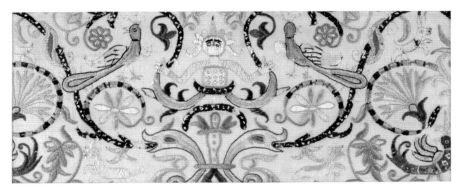

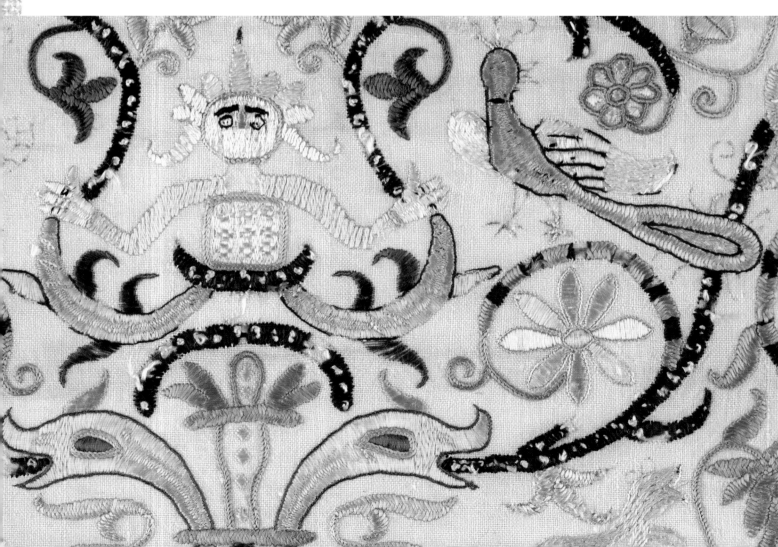

CHINESE HANGING

TECHNIQUE: silk embroidery
DATE: 19th century
PLACE of origin: China
SIZE: 97 x 96cm (38¼ x 37¾in)

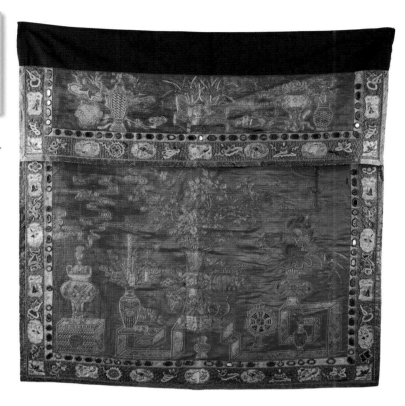

We go to China for the final page in this chapter and a hanging with a beautifully embroidered border of realistic birds enclosed in compartments, and surrounded by flowers. The peacock is in peacock blue silk thread and, although looking rather wild eyed, he is striding confidently through the landscape (bottom left). Notice how big his feet are. The heron stands in water and looks quizzically backwards (bottom right).

The embroidery in the compartments is all in silk thread and straight stitches, but notice the strip of mirror glass above the birds. Here the mirrors are surrounded by a metal mount, which is stitched to the background, unlike Indian shisha embroidery where the glass is held in place entirely with thread. There are intricate designs in couched metal thread on the border and on the main part of the panel. The border, which could be a later addition to the piece, is hand stitched to the rest of the panel. This panel was gifted to the Embroiderers' Guild in 1970.

Embroiderers' Guild number: EG3809

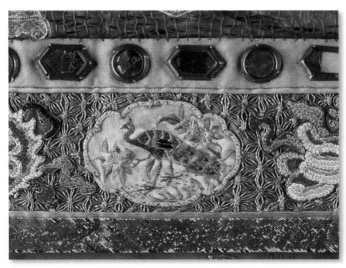

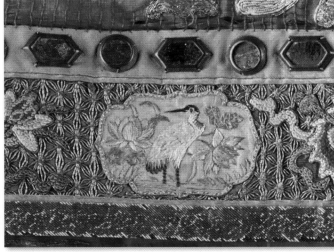

STITCHES AND
MORE STITCHES

In this chapter we cover some techniques not seen yet in this book, such as three-dimensional birds and an owl in leather appliqué. Most, however, are techniques we have looked at before. We come across a cushion cover dedicated to ducks and domestic items in the form of a tea cosy, stool cover and a cot blanket. The Parrot and Grapes panel is another example of beautiful silk embroidery. Finally in this chapter, and linking to the next book in the series, is an example of early 20th century textile art by Elizabeth Grace Thomson.

CHAIN STITCH LETTER CASE

TECHNIQUE: chain stitch
DATE: 19th century
PLACE of origin: Scandinavia
SIZE: 11 x 63cm (4¼ x 24¾in)

Here is a series of lovely little birds positioned on the pockets of what is described as a letter case. They appear in pairs, facing each other on either side of a flower, as though they are protecting the rather stylized tulip between them.

The letter case has a black fabric background and the embroidery uses wool thread worked entirely in chain stitch. I particularly like the muted colours of these birds against a black background, which enhances the design.

This piece is chain stitch with a needle, worked on the front of the embroidery, compared to the tambour embroidery we saw earlier where the chain stitch is made using a hook from the back of the fabric.

Embroiderers' Guild number: EG5192

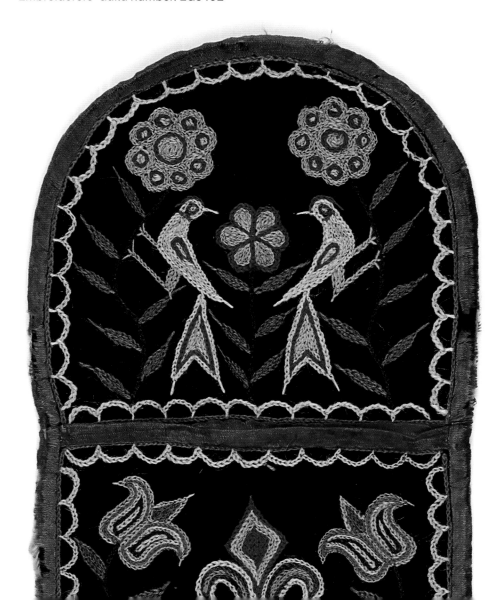

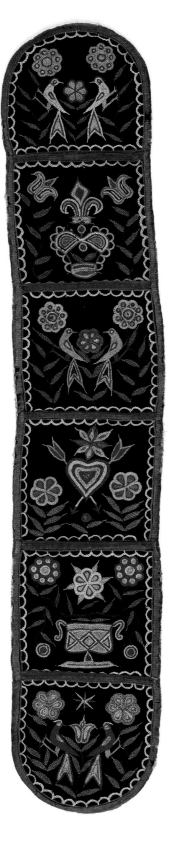

TENT STITCH STOOL COVER

TECHNIQUE: canvas work, tent stitch

DATE: 1963

PLACE of origin: Great Britain

SIZE: 34 x 41cm (13½ x 16in)

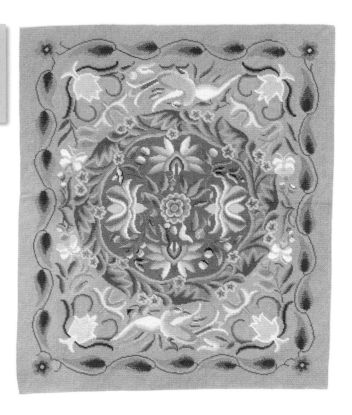

Here is an example of an embroidery that we know little about. It is described as a stool top and is embroidered in tent stitch with wool threads on a canvas background.

The colours are muted as in the letter case opposite, but the effect is very different. This is a busy design where the elements get lost in the pale background because background and threads are similarly pale. The one element that does stand out is the border of red leaves. I believe this design was purchased as a printed canvas. There are two birds – mirror images of each other – that might be swans, at either end of the design.

Maker: Mrs Brand
Gifted by: Mrs Brand
Embroiderers' Guild number: EG1760

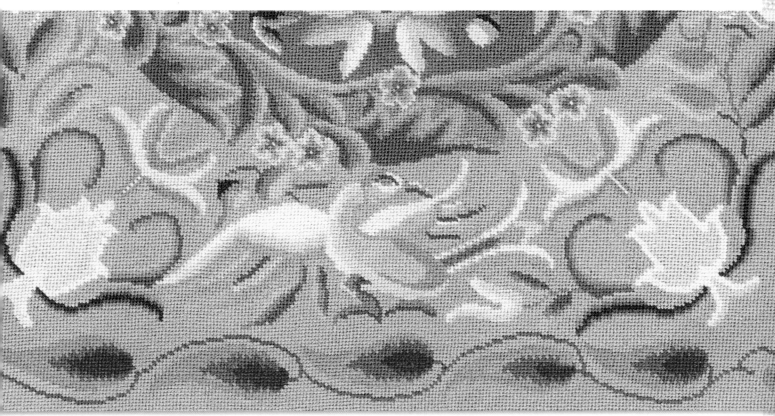

SILK EMBROIDERY SEAT COVER

TECHNIQUE: silk embroidery
DATE: 1900–1910
PLACE of origin: Great Britain
SIZE: 36 x 28cm (14¼ x 11in)

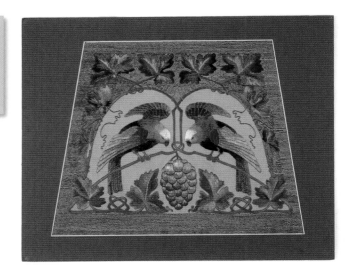

This panel is described as a chair seat in an early exhibition catalogue. If so, it must have been for a decorative rather than functional chair, as the beautiful silk floss embroidery would have soon worn away.

Two parrots are perched on a vine branch, flapping their wings and looking with interest at a bunch of grapes. The ground fabric is a green, furnishing satin and the threads are untwisted floss silk. The background features couched threads and the parrots are stitched in long and short stitch. Split stitch and satin stitch can be seen in parts of the design. The piece was gifted to the Embroiderers' Guild Collection in 1964.

Embroiderers' Guild number: EG2022

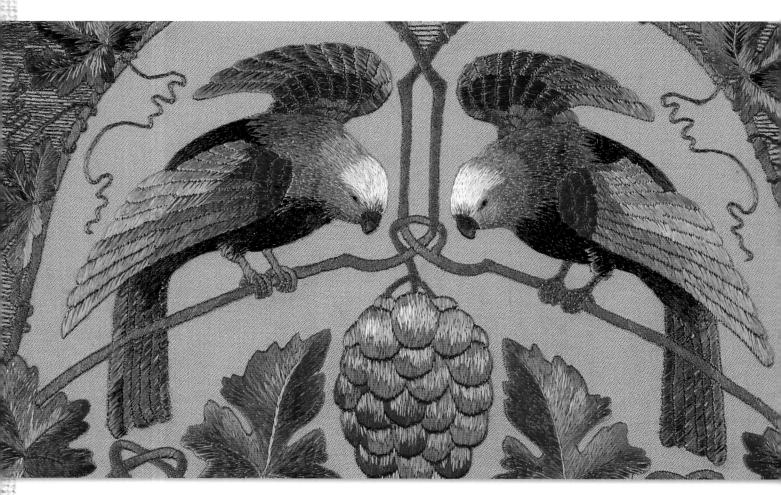

WOOLLEN COT COVER

TECHNIQUE: hand embroidery
DATE: 1952
PLACE of origin: Great Britain
SIZE: 75 x 58cm (29½ x 23in)

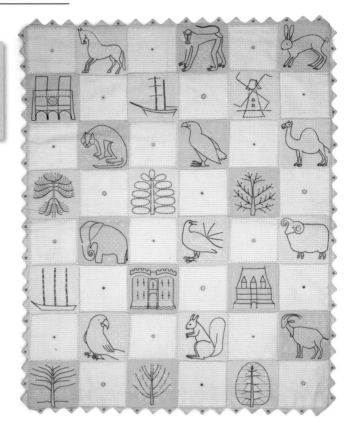

This charming cot cover is a patchwork of fine woollen fabric, stitched with cotton thread in chain and herringbone stitches. It was made for the Needlework Development Scheme, which was formed to encourage good design and technique. Embroideries were circulated to schools and colleges for study purposes. Starting with art colleges in Scotland in 1934, it spread to England where it flourished until its closure in 1960.

The simplicity of the design of this cot cover will appeal to beginners. The birds are outlined in dark blue thread and white threads have been used to fill in details of feathers and a background of leaves. This piece was donated to the Embroiderers' Guild Collection in 1962.

Embroiderers' Guild number: EG1055

DUCK CUSHION COVER

TECHNIQUE: blackwork filling stitches
DATE: 20th century
PLACE of origin: Great Britain
SIZE: 35cm (13¾in) in diameter

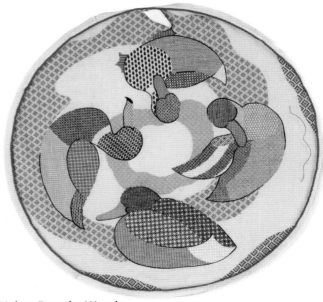

This cushion cover is a recent acquisition to the Embroiderers' Guild Collection. The birds are clearly ducks circling around in a pond. I am very fond of ducks and this piece portrays their characteristics beautifully, preening their feathers and floating happily on the water.

One of the ducks is a male mallard. The other three might be females. The stitches are all filling stitches characteristic of blackwork, but in this case several colours have been used, giving the cover a modern look in comparison to the traditional monochrome of blackwork. The maker is Dorothy Wood, who personally donated her cushion to the Collection. The background fabric is an evenweave cotton fabric and the threads are also cotton.

Maker: Dorothy Wood
Gifted by: Dorothy Wood
Embroiderers' Guild number: EG3856

JANE LEMON'S HEN

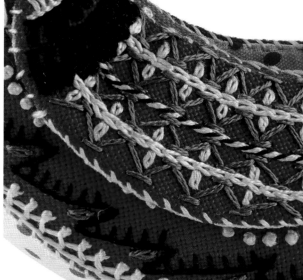

TECHNIQUE: 3D birds
DATE: 1973
PLACE of origin: Great Britain
SIZE: 18 x 15cm (7 x 6in)

Not all embroideries in the Embroiderers' Guild Collection are historical or examples of contemporary textile art and during the mid 20th century, toys and three-dimensional birds and animals were popular, often decorated with intricate embroidery. Some examples were made for the Needlework Development Scheme, which we heard about in the cot cover in this chapter. This hen, made of striped cotton fabric and with a leather beak and comb, wears a hessian (burlap) shawl and a necklace of knotted thread with a plastic jewel. Her eye is a felt circle attached with a bead.

Maker: Jane Lemon

Embroiderers' Guild number: EG4498

Jane Lemon MBE, who died in 2015, was a well-respected teacher, author and member of the Embroiderers' Guild. Originally a costume designer for the BBC and theatre, she turned to ecclesiastical embroidery and in 1978 formed the Sarum Group, affiliated to a Guild branch, to produce textiles for Salisbury Cathedral. Many examples of her ecclesiastical work can be seen in churches and cathedrals in the UK and America.

FELT BIRD

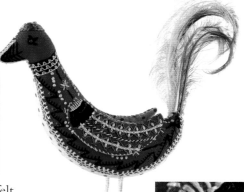

TECHNIQUE: 3D bird, hand embroidery
DATE: mid 20th century
PLACE of origin: Great Britain
SIZE: 18 x 15cm (7 x 6in)

This little bird is made from firmly stuffed felt, with wrapped wire legs and feet and has feathers for a tail. The eyes are made from tiny felt shapes attached with a bead and the threads used are cotton. Embroidery is in chain stitch, blanket stitch, stem stitch and feather stitch with French knots. This bird is characteristic of the work of Winsome Douglass, author of classic books on toy making and a contributor to the Needlework Development Scheme.

Maker: Winsome Douglass
Embroiderers' Guild number: EG3674

LEATHER APPLIQUÉ OWL

TECHNIQUE: leather appliqué with hand embroidery

DATE: 20th century

PLACE of origin: Great Britain

SIZE: 20 x 15cm (8 x 6in)

This is an interesting depiction of an owl perched on a branch. Little is known about it as it was purchased at an antiques fair and the dealer did not have any information about it. The fabrics used appear to be furnishing fabrics with suede leather. The branch and leaves are all applied leather shapes with hand stitching and the owl's wing is padded fabric with leather pieces stitched over the top.

The embroidery is in cotton thread with French knots, satin stitch, feather stitch and couched threads. The eye is made from cut metal plate with straight stitches and beads, the beak is applied leather and the end of the tail is decorated with a row of bugle beads, which are small, coloured tubes of glass. Notice how the feathers have been made with loops of straight stitches and then embellished with beads and stitches in a darker thread.

This piece is on loan to the Embroiderers' Guild Collection

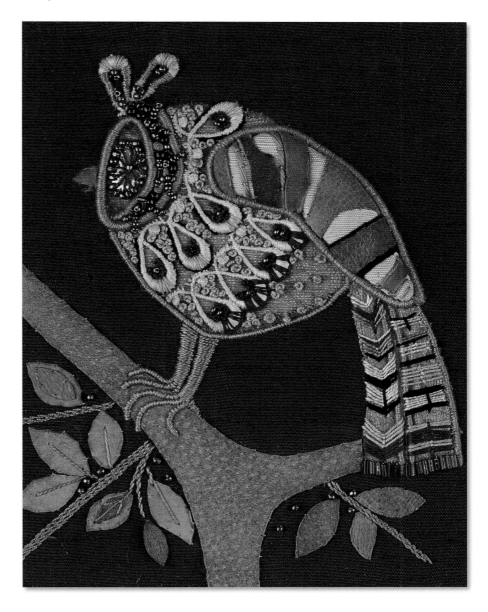

TEA COSY

TECHNIQUE: hand embroidery
DATE: 20th century (1915)
PLACE of origin: Great Britain
SIZE: 19 x 12cm (7½ x 4¾in)

The Embroiderers' Guild has a large collection of tea cosies from the 19th century to the present day. This tea cosy is hand embroidered on cotton with cotton threads and portrays a flock of birds flying round a bird bath with a background of trees in a landscape. The embroidery is worked in long and short stitch.

Maker: Dorothea Nield, who was a tutor at the Royal School of Needlework.
Embroiderers' Guild number: EG3514

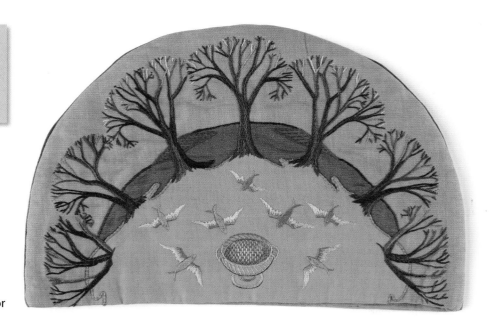

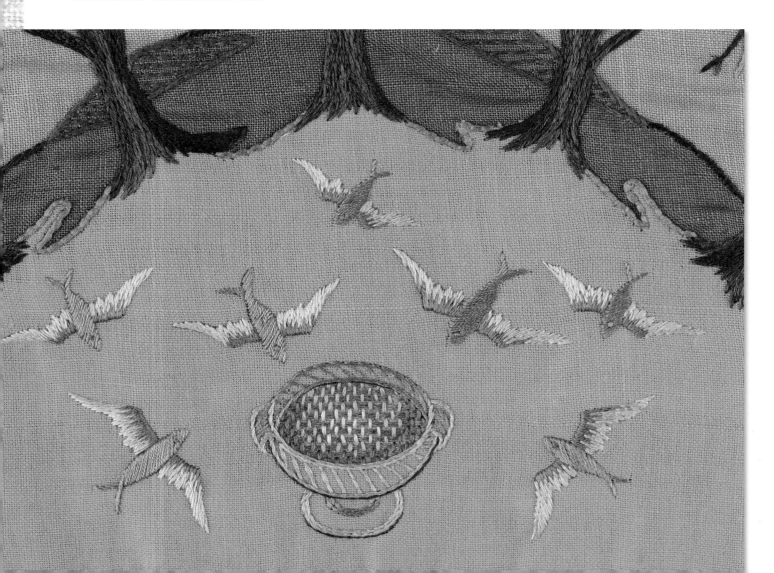

THE BLUE BIRD

TECHNIQUE: hand embroidery
DATE: 1931
PLACE of origin: Great Britain
SIZE: 35 x 35cm (13¾ x 13¾in)

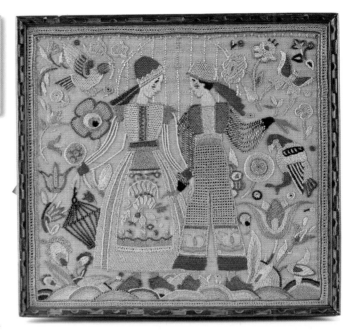

'The Blue Bird' was first exhibited at the Arts and Crafts Exhibition Society in London, 1932, when it was described as peasant-like in design and contemporary in outlook. The background is a woollen fabric and the thread is a lightly twisted silk. Stitches used include Italian cross, Greek cross filling, buttonhole, backstitch and whipped chain with some couched threads.

There are two birds: the blue bird itself, which appears to have escaped from its cage, and a parrot. Take a look back at the Noah's Ark panels on page 97. Notice the animals on the panels, which link to the next book in the series, *Embroidered Treasures: Animals*.

Maker: Elizabeth Grace Thompson (1895–1981), embroiderer and teacher, who became head of Bromley College of Art, UK
Bequest of: Elizabeth Grace Thompson in 1982
Embroiderers' Guild number: EG1983.109

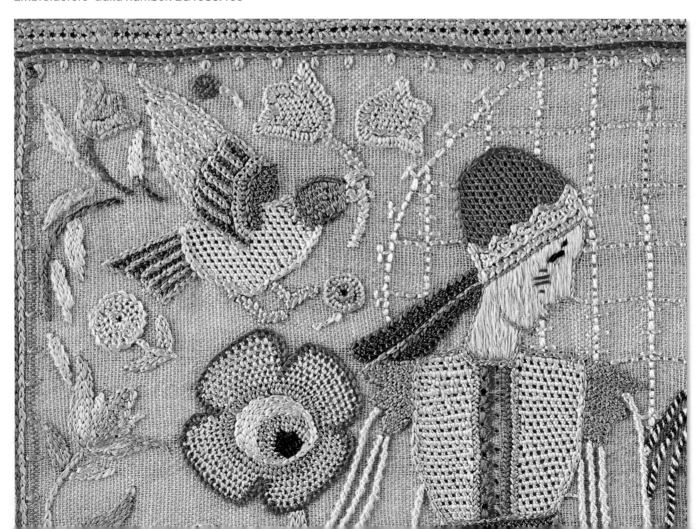

INDEX